NORTHAMPT

FOLK
TALES

NORTHAMPTONSHIRE

FOLK TALES

KEVAN MANWARING

The History Press

Dedicated to all my friends and family in Northamptonshire.

First published 2013

The History Press
The Mill, Brimscombe Port
Stroud, Gloucestershire, GL5 2QG
www.thehistorypress.co.uk

British Library Cataloguing in Publication Data.
A catalogue record for this book is available from the British Library.

ISBN 978 0 7524 6788 7

Typesetting and origination by The History Press
Printed in Great Britain

CONTENTS

ACKNOWLEDGEMENTS

Thank you to Northampton Central Library; The History Press; Justin and Penny; Jimtom; Robert Goodman; and the good folk of Northamptonshire, past and present.

All illustrations are by the author.

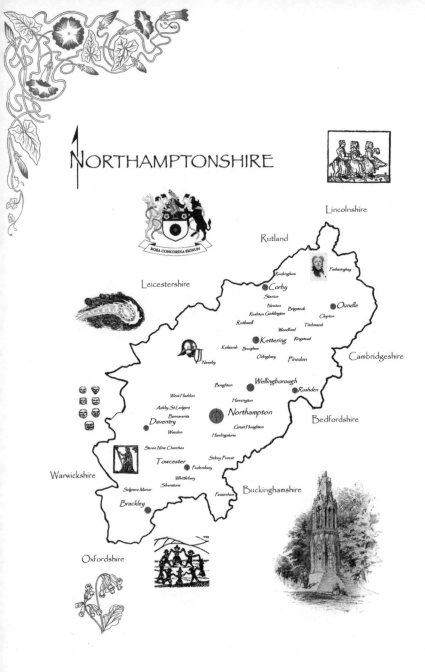

Northamptonshire

Lincolnshire

Rutland

Leicestershire

Rockingham

Fotheringhay

Corby

Stanion

Newton

Brigstock

Oundle

Rushton Geddington

Clopton

Rothwell

Titchmarsh

Woodford

Kettering

Ringstead

Kelmarsh

Broughton

Orlingbury

Finedon

Naseby

Cambridgeshire

Boughton

Wellingborough

Rushden

West Haddon

Hannington

Ashby St Ledgers

Bannaventa

Northampton

Daventry

Bedfordshire

Weedon

Great Houghton

Hardingstone

Stowe Nine Churches

Towcester

Salcey Forest

Paulerspury

Whittlebury

Silverstone

Sulgrave Manor

Passenham

Brackley

Buckinghamshire

Warwickshire

Oxfordshire

ROSA CONCORDIA SIGNUM

INTRODUCTION

As a young man growing up in Northampton, the town of my birth felt, on the surface, to be the most disenchanted place on Earth. Of course, with my limited experience of the world I had little to compare it to (there are, undoubtedly, worse places, and there are better) but as a young man it felt pretty grim. A rundown post-industrial town in the 1980s was not a happy place to be. However, this was as much to do with my adolescent angst as it was to do with the state of the nation.

Yet, as a child I found enchantment in my neck of the woods. I had grown up on the doorstep of Delapré Abbey, a twelfth-century Clunaic nunnery, a former family home, and, at that time, the County Record Office. I visited its wilderness gardens every day, taking my dog and my imagination for a walk. It was here, daydreaming amongst the oaks, that my storytelling started, stirred by tales of witches and gypsies, grey ladies and ghostly queens.

Surrounding the abbey were woods, fields and a lake known as 'The Gravel Pits'. These too were assimilated into my fledgling mythic landscape. Queen Eleanor's Cross stood at the top of the London Road, and beyond that were the edges of my world: Hardingstone, Wootton, Milton Malsor, Stoke Bruene, and further, Salcey Forest – places I explored on cycle rides with my brother.

An Iron-Age hill fort, Hunsbury Hill, loomed large on the horizon – another important borderplace, and my first taste of the prehistoric. It thrilled me that in such a prosaic, colonised, cement-smothered place, a remnant of the ancient world survived. But there were other rags and tatters of the distant past – fragments of bigger stories, hiding in plain sight.

I remember playing amongst the excavation of a Roman villa by my grandparents' house on Briar Hill (where, it turns out, a Neolithic settlement was discovered). St Peters, by the train station, is a Saxon church made of exquisite corbel-stones with a mysterious carved slab inside. The railway station itself used to be called Castle Station, but all that remains of Northampton Castle (the setting for Shakespeare's *King John*) is the postern gate and some ramparts. St Seps, as we called The Church of the Holy Sepulchre, an eleventh-century church on the north side of town, is one of four remaining round churches built by the Knights Templar, the powerful Crusaders, on their return from the Holy Land.

Other quiet wonders of the town's past waited to be discovered, but these were what I was aware of growing up in the town. The old fleapit on the Market Square, then later, the ABC Cinema, at the top of the high street, were just as important; as were obscure newsagents, tucked away in backstreets, where I would trek on foot in the hope of finding American comic books that my local shop didn't stock. My burgeoning imagination was like a pyre that needed feeding. It consumed stories in any form it could find – TV serials, movie tie-ins, cartoons, superhero comics, paperbacks. Ravenous for narrative, I started to create my own, first in comic strips with friends, then 'scenarios' for roleplaying games. I enjoyed writing short stories in English. My Secondary School English teacher, Mr Alsop, was a great orator, and would proclaim on his favourite subjects of Bruce Springsteen and Rugby at the drop of a hat. He ran Tunnels and Trolls gaming sessions at lunchtime. Through his avuncular manner and enthusiasm, he made his classes popular and the study of English Literature enjoyable. I recall vividly the reaction of a story I wrote on the subject of 'School Reunion', which was read out in class by Mr Alsop. It made everyone laugh and for the first time I realised my stories could entertain, that perhaps I had a gift worth nurturing (until then I had hid in the art room, where my drawing skills enabled me to shine amid the thuggish delinquency of a sink-school comprehensive).

I was shy and awkward and a bit solitary – happier in my own company, although never 'alone' in nature, for my imagination populated it with the stuff of my dreams.

It wasn't until Art College (initially Nene College, as it was called then, St George's Campus on the Racecourse) that I began to find myself and grow into my skin, a skin that had felt ill-fitting until then. I had felt out of place in my home, my neighbourhood, my school, my era. Who was I and where did I belong? It took me most of my twenties to work that out – I was drawn to the West Country, to a brighter land of stone circles and summer festivals. I made my home in Bath, where I became Bard of the City after winning a local contest. I had found myself and somewhere I belonged – a community I could be myself in.

Yet, I kept my connection to Northampton, honouring old friendships. I started an annual gathering in a local woodland, to bring my old and new friends together – mingling old and new stories.

After graduating from art college, I returned to Northampton and, for a couple of years, I worked on my first novel, about a haunted tree – an ancient beech tree hidden in a corner of a car park – set over a thousand years of the town's dark history. I undertook extensive research for this, spending many hours in the Local Studies Section of the Central Library. I was partly motivated by wanting to understand why the town was the way it was ('The dark heart of England', as I termed it at the time). Learning its story I broke free of it – I was no longer controlled by its narrative. I discovered many hidden treasures in the process of writing that book (still unpublished). I learnt to appreciate my old hometown and mourn for its former glory, what it once was, and what it could have been. I stumbled on the legend of Ragener (whose name means 'born of the people's strength') and I imagined a sleeping giant, the dormant potential of the town, the king-in-the-land waiting to wake up. I found that king in Bath, in the form of legendary Bladud. In a way, it was my own latent 'kingliness'.

Northampton had kept him slumbering, as though spellbound. The town was like a kingdom placed under a spell and enshrouded in thorns. In truth, they were my own as much as anything.

When I returned there years later it felt like the town had finally 'woken up'. There was a new energy in the place. It seemed to me as though the locals had found their civic pride, and were appreciating what they had under their feet.

Shoe Town had found its soul.

Some friends of mine started the Bardic Picnic at Delapré Abbey, after consulting me about the Bardic Chair of Bath, which I had become part of, and I was invited to judge the contest and perform there. It felt like I was coming full circle. Something healed. I was delighted to see local storytellers, poets and musicians step up and shine. There was a great local scene, encouraged by regular open mic nights (e.g. Raising the Awen). The town had never looked or felt better. It was being re-enchanted by those who live there.

The process of collecting and writing these folk tales has been a moving experience. It has made me revisit my old haunts with new eyes; as well as explore nooks and crannies of the county that had so far eluded me, on my Triumph Legend motorbike, wearing my 'folk tale goggles'. Northamptonshire is a beautiful county, which justly deserves its name as the 'Rose of the Shires'. In sleepy villages, legends have wandered – figures from myth and history: Boudicca; St Patrick; Robin Hood; Mary Queen of Scots; Eleanor of Aquitaine; Thomas a Becket; Hereward the Wake; Oliver Cromwell; Captain Slash; Crick and Watson. Although I knew a few of the tales, I was impressed by the many more I found. I was spoilt for choice, and have included only a selection – fuller narratives, as opposed to the countless scraps of folklore to be found in old tomes. I have opted for tales that will 'work' in the oral fashion, and have shaped them to this end. As a young man I was disheartened that there seemed, on the surface, to be no 'good stories' about the county. Anything interesting seemed to happen elsewhere. Nothing famous or successful or beautiful seemed to come out of the town. Now I know that's not to be true. I have rediscovered a county filled with magic and wonders and rattling yarns.

Such tales mythologise a landscape – as I did as a child in my neck of the woods – and ultimately can help re-enchant it, by shifting perceptions. If a local tale helps people feel that where they live is special, then they will appreciate it even more.

When a place finds its story again, it finds its soul.

Northamptonshire is an amazing county, filled to the brim with heritage and a remarkable history. There are many hidden gems to be found amid its quiet charms. I hope this collection whets your appetite and encourages you to go looking for them.

Kevan Manwaring, 2013

THE
GREEN ABBEY

By salmon wisdom I am ever returning
along that avenue of gothic oaks,
towards the white clock tower, still,
above the bolted coach-house.

Perambulating about
this accumulation of architecture:
the sandstone hourglass
of my memory mansion.
The crackle of gravel
my favourite track
of this old record office –
familiar grooves spiralling inward.

Into the dog-eared garden,
passed the gravestones of pets:
the ghost of my hound leading me on –
playing with me still in his paradise.
So many times he brought me here,
teaching me to follow my instincts,
to listen to nature,
nurturing my fledgling wild-self –
the boypuppy who became a wolf.

Here in a personal wilderness
I found solace
from the pain of passion,
first and lost loves,
alienation and aloneness.

Discovering solitude
but unable to share its bliss.

In make-believe I found my beloved;
playmates in hide-and-seek with passers-by:
a Jack-in-the-Green, without knowing why.

In this nursery of my imagination
I learnt the alphabet of trees, an Adam
naming them octopus heart monkey.
By a foetid pond with broken maw
I cast a witch in shadowy hut;
and gypsy lights winked
in the gloaming;
and grey ladies drifted
in the undead night –
the phantom nuns
who left a legacy of peace
as they paced their sanctuary:
every step a prayer.

And here I repair when I grow weary of the world
for their healing grace –
a taste of the grail
that restores my wasteland

with the memory of summer,
of sunfat days of timeless youth,
of picnics for virgin palates,
of blind kisses beneath staring stars,

and shadowdancing
under champagne moons.

Where goddesses of fish and cat
enticed from their fastnesses
I gleaned an inkling of the Muse.

And in the grove of my Lord and Lady
I silently communed, vertebrae to bark.
Above, tall and strong,
how they watched me grow –
their heartwood my Axis Mundi:
spine of my history.
Each ring witnessing my full circle –
as past and future pilgrims
rendezvoused with déjà vu
beneath the trysting tree.

O, the oaks of my Arcadia,
archive of my life,
endure always –
keep the world at bay.

As in amber be the bowers
of blessed Delapré.

ONE

THE GREY LADY OF DELAPRÉ

She always appears at dusk. Walking the grounds in a long grey robe, or is it only the colour-sapping moonlight that makes it appear so? For others would swear it was blue. And is that white, or an unearthly light about her? She looks sad – though that is gauged more from posture than expression. Those unfortunate enough to have glimpsed her face – a vision that paralysed them with fear –

said her eyes were orbless pits of shadow. Did she make a sound? No, she was as silent as the grave, gliding noiselessly over the gravel paths. A smudge of grey against grey, caught in the corner of your eye. A trick of the moonlight, surely? Your imagination running away with you, as you take the dog for an evening walk around the abbey grounds, not a soul in sight. Then, there she is – at the end of the path. Waiting. But, by the time you are there – nothing. Sometimes, she has been glimpsed inside the house – when it used to be a Records Office; or, before that, used by the War Office. A soft figure at the foot of the stairs: a sudden coolness. If the last owners of the house knew of her, they kept it to themselves. Miss Mary Bouverie lived there for twenty-six years before being ousted by the War Office. She moved back after a two-year exile in Duston on the other side of town. She moved to a room above the stable block but died within a year. What had she known? Perhaps seeing her beloved Delapré overrun with servicemen and women was the death of her? Or maybe it made someone else turn in the grave? Someone used to conflict – to seeing its harsh realities up close hand …

'O God, by whose grace thy servants, the Holy Abbots of Cluny, enkindled with the fire of thy love, became burning and shining lights in thy Church: Grant that we also may be aflame with the spirit of love and discipline, and may ever walk before thee as children of light; through Jesus Christ our Lord, who with thee, in the unity of the Holy Spirit, liveth and reigneth, one God, now and forever.'

The nun finished her orisons and got to her feet – a little more nimbly than some of the elder sisters. At seventeen she was the youngest of them. While some were in the autumn or winter of their years, she was in the bloom of life – as brimming with beauty as the grounds of the abbey on a glorious morning in July, a swoon of flowers swaying in the light warm breeze – pollen slowly spiralling in the shards of sun that penetrated the bowers that no man may ever walk: a paradise for bees. The Abbey of Mary of the Meadow was walled off from the world of men – a sanctuary, a refuge, an oasis of calm sanity in a kingdom turned mad with war, a war between, of all things, roses.

And now the tide of madness had come to them; was lapping at their door.

She did not know much of the world, for she was cloistered here at a young age. An unnatural fate for a young woman on the brink of life, perhaps, but it was the only chance of education, of leading a life of mind and spirit, beyond the disease-ridden and back-breaking grind of reality for most in her village. It had been thrown to her like a lifeline but now she regretted it. Prone to hasty actions, which she always seemed to regret later, she was hoping this Clunaic life would curb this tendency – certainly the Abbess did.

Gonora Downghton held no truck with fools, and sniffed out her wayward tendencies straight away: 'Here at Delapré, there is no place for hasty actions, for rash words, for a young girl's foolishness – only hard work. The Devil will not find your hands idle.' And nor did he, what with all the endless prayers, washing, cooking, cleaning, gardening, mending, polishing and so on. And so the diurnal round of prayer, work, and sleep became her world. There were moments of snatched conversations with some of the more gregarious sisters – moments soon hushed by a frosty stare, a finger to the lips, or a stifled snigger as the Abbess or one of her lieutenants passed.

Sometimes the sisters would talk of their lives before taking the cloth, and the young nun would patch together a strange warped map of life beyond the cloisters – a land dominated by cruel and lustful men. She had only known her father and brothers, who were kind enough, in their gruff, cubbish way – but this talk of dark and dangerous figures thrilled her, she was ashamed to realise. Failure to mention it in confession compounded her shame, but made it even more potent. Her dark fantasies possessed her day and night, but now her shadowy desires were about to burst into daylight.

Something heavy crashed through the foliage towards her. Lost in her dreaming world, she was unable to react in time – freezing instead as a mangled, mailed body erupted from the bushes and landed splayed at her feet. The stench of blood, piss and sweat rose to her nostrils. The shredded tunic he wore over his coat of chain-mail was soaked in mud, obscuring the colours beneath. A rusty sword had fallen by his side, buckled by warfare. He twitched in agony, gargling a crimson froth; his body mottled by the spiked signatures of morning stars.

A soldier! One of the dark and dangerous!

Yet the truth was far uglier than her fantasy. His helmet, a battered bowl-shaped affair, had fallen off in his writhing, to reveal a pug-nosed, gap-toothed man, face smeared with the grime of battle. Between each rasp of breath, he seemed to call out the name of someone, barely discernible.

She could feel no desire for this alien figure prostrate before her, only a curious pity. What kind of world had he come from, to end like this? As if in answer, her ears discerned a foreign sound shattering the deep peace of the abbey gardens.

She could make out the distorted sounds of war cries and the 'chink' of steel, unpredictable cannon fire punctuated the proceedings, confirming the scenario and causing her heart to beat wildly. Like a panicked animal, she fled – but in her confusion she ran towards, not away, from the source.

She came to the edge of the gardens, to the rear gate which led out to the adjacent farm. In the distance on the hill sat the town overlooking the winding Nene, which flowed between the town and abbey, as though cutting off her sacred world from the secular. Many a time had she wandered the banks, daydreaming of the life beyond; but today – the sun burning off the mist over the willowed banks and serried ranks of reeds – the peaceful meadows depicted a different scene, which took her breath: towards the river there was a seething phalanx of troops, thousands of them – more men than she reckoned lived in the world.

Amid the havoc she could not tell which side was which: it was a frantic scrimmage of mud-bound psychotics, cap-a-pie in the mortal clay which the water meadow had churned up as the thronging thousands passed over it. White-rosed regiments swarmed down from the ridge south of the abbey – a bristling arsenal held aloft as they charged like trees swept by storm waters – around the nunnery, the tempest's eye, towards the dug-in enemy, seemingly impenetrable behind a thorn-wall of stakes and ditches. Betwixt mounds of earth, poked the smouldering snouts of cannons, though few of the gunners, it seemed, could light their damp powder as well as their fellow bowmen could shoot their plagues of arrows, which cut heavily into the ranks of attacking horsemen; those that managed to navigate their distraught steeds over the defences dismounted and hacked or were hacked down. Ragged banners rose and fell like sails on a squally sea. The pendants of the red rose flapped in the distance among the tents which backed onto the river – an extravagant marquee, which could only have been the Royal Pavilion, among them.

Now she recalled what one of the sisters had said about this 'War of the Roses' in explanation to her naive question: 'Cousin fights against cousin for the throne.'

Why would anyone do this to one another, let alone cousins?

Soldiers slipped in the churned up mud, fell on their weapons or dropped them in the fray; horses panicked and trampled infantry; men wept for their fallen comrades or cowered in terror. Occasionally, a foot-soldier was ejected from the scrum and was either pushed back in by the sergeant-at-arms or, if too badly injured, gathered up by her fellow nuns in their distinctive blue robes – orbiting the fracas like Valkyries. Two at a time, they helped carry the walking wounded back to Delapré, or administered aid where they fell. The dead, or dying, they lifted with difficulty into carts, which, when full, were trundled back to the abbey. The slaughter assailed her from all sides: bodies clogged the stream; their iron-blood irrigated the flowerbeds; weapons took root where they were plunged into the soft soil; dropped or discarded armour was scattered like scales upon the downy lawn.

She was jolted from her stunned reverie by a sister, who scolded her into action. She joined the others, tending to the wounded.

The day passed in a blur of sweat and blood.

She can't remember when she fell asleep – like many of her sisters, she had slept on a pew, too dog-tired to care at its hardness; their beds given over to the worst cases.

In the morning, her new nursing duties resumed. The abbey had become a hospital. There was an eerie silence in the fields beyond – she heard that three hundred and fifty thousand men had fought, and that three hundred Lancastrians lay dead. The King was captured and held prisoner overnight in the abbey by the victors. His Queen had fled north, to Scotland. This had been disclosed by the Archbishop of Canterbury no less, who had watched the battle and then her flight from the hill of the Headless Cross. All this was gleaned in breathless exchanges between the exhausting rounds of the makeshift wards. Here, both sides were tended to – though priority and the best beds were offered to the victors. The Lancastrian soldiers were terrified of what would happen to them. The Abbess assured them that while under her roof no harm would come to them. All were God's children and would receive all the care and comfort that could offer.

There was one who caught the young sister's eye – a dark-haired Lancastrian. He must have been, what, nineteen? He had been frightened at first, but had tried his best not to show it, yet in his pain he had called out to his mother. She had dabbed his brow with a cool, damp cloth and had cleaned his wounds as best she could. It was the first time she had seen a man's body up close, beyond her brothers and father – who didn't count (as familiar to her as her own flesh). She avoided his gaze – those deep, dark orbs – as she tended to him. She could feel his gaze burning into her and it made her cheeks glow.

'What's your name?' His voice, with its tang of the Dales, startled her.

'Ellie,' she said quietly. She had been named after Eleanor, the Queen of the Cross, who had lain here in this very abbey on her way to London, and a cross had been raised in her honour. When it had lost its cross, no one knew for certain though everyone had their theory. It was known locally as the Headless Cross. It had been a familiar landmark to her, growing up on the edge of town. And now it felt like she was losing her head!

'Help me,' he whispered. He gripped her forearm and forced her to look at him. With. Those. Eyes. 'They will slaughter us as soon as we leave your walls. As soon as we can walk they will march us to our doom. An execution in some quiet glade. Out of sight, out of mind. Far less expensive than feeding and guarding prisoners. I've heard the horrors they commit in the name of their cause. Help me escape – this very night. At least I will have more of a chance than the poor sods who cannot stand.'

She chewed her lip, then nodded.

In her mind flashed a plan – she would flee with him. They would elope – like lovers in a story – and live together as man and woman should, until the end of their days. There would be children and animals; a small farm somewhere. A simple, contented life.

She slipped away and prepared a bag of her few possessions. She managed to scavenge some food – some would say steal – from the kitchens. And then, in the dead of night, when all were asleep, exhausted from the day's travails, she went to him and quietly, painfully, she helped him out of bed. They carried his boots and his bloodstained tunic, rolled up in a bundle. The ward-sister stirred and turned. They froze. But she resumed her snoring.

And they were out in the gardens – using a secret way through the cellar she knew was unguarded by the Lancastrians. A couple of soldiers played dice around a fire, coarsely laughing.

In the darkness, they sneaked passed and made their way to the back entrance. The moon was half-full and gave them some light, but not too much, so it was easy to hog the shadows. Ellie's heart beat fast, her knees nearly gave way, but the young soldier held her hand which gave her courage. She couldn't believe this was happening. It was like a story. She tingled all over. It was as though she had been asleep, but now she had woken up. Awake in the middle of the night. It was like a dream …

Suddenly, there was a sound. Heavy footsteps coming along the path. They turned to hide – to dart into the undergrowth – but it was too late. Two guards were before them, blocking their way. The farm gate was just behind them. So close. But it might as well be another world.

'Halt! Who goes there?'

'It's one of the Lancastrian dogs, doing a moonlight flit. Taking one of the nuns with him too, the cur!' They thrust their pikes forward – lunged at the soldier.

It all happened so slowly, so fast. Ellie screamed and leapt in front of him. Rash. It would be her undoing.

It was. She looked down and a pike stuck through her belly – impregnating her with death. The soldier cried out, reached for her, but was butted to the ground. Her gaze rolled upwards to the half-moon. It turned crimson, like a cup of dark wine.

His name. She didn't even know his name.

Ellie was buried outside the nuns' burial ground – the inner garden; a little plot on one corner of the abbey grounds, a sad dismal spot underneath a yew tree. There her mortal remains rested, but not her soul – tormented by the brutal nature of her death and her lost love, she took to wandering the grounds in search of him. Sometimes, she would go to the bottom of the stairs – hoping he would appear and take her away.

But he never came.

He had met his fate, with the rest.

The War of the Roses ended. Others conflicts swept the land as the centuries past. The abbey was handed over to Henry VIII by the last Abbess, Clementina Stock. The next year, 1539, the Tate Family bought it and their descendants lived there for two centuries. Other owners came and went. Time passed, yet the peacefulness of Delapré remained – a green sanctuary still in a chaotic world. Something of the atmosphere of the nunnery lingers – an odour of sanctity. A phantom trace of the past.

And Eleanor, the Grey Lady of Delapré, walks the grounds of the abbey to this day.

In this story I have taken a fragment of folklore – about the Grey Lady of Delapré Abbey – and imagined the 'backstory', using the major historical landmark of the Battle of Northampton, as it became known, which took place on 10 July 1460. A Clunaic Nunnery (one of only two in England), it was built by Simon de Senlis, the founder of Northampton, in 1145. I grew up just over the London Road from Delapré Abbey and would go there at least once a day, walking my beloved dog, a Welsh Border Collie. It was, and is, a very special place for me – 'The nursery of my imagination' as I call it (in my poem 'The Green Abbey'). This is where I learnt to daydream and also to connect with nature. My life as a storyteller started here. I remember going on walks there with my Dad and our pack of dogs (two or three). His favourite time was at night and he would use it to wind me up by saying the lights through the trees (in fact lamp-posts) were gypsy lanterns, ready to snatch me away. Or that the Grey Lady would get me. A hut in the gardens became, in my fertile childhood imagination, the witch's hut. Trees were given their own names – the Monkey Tree; the Octopus Tree; the Heart Tree. The place lent itself to such make-believe. Now, it hosts the Bardic Picnic every summer – an annual contest for the best storyteller, poet or singer in the town, partly inspired by my involvement in the Bardic Chair of Caer Badon. I was asked to judge and perform at the first contest, returning as a professional storyteller. The Friends of Delapré Abbey look after it now, keeping it in the hands of the community, having fought off bids by the golf course, and others who wish to turn it into something residential and exclusive. It remains an important sanctuary for all in the town: its green heart.

Two

The
Glass Fort

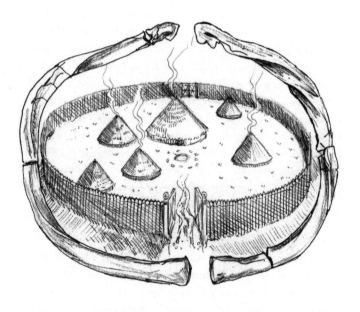

The boy cycled through the graffiti-stained underpass on his Chopper, hollering the theme tune of *Doctor Who*, his favourite show, to himself. What would Tom Baker make of this time tunnel, as he and his few friends thought of it? It led to Hunsbury Hill – the old hill fort on the edge of the estate – the only 'hill' on this side of the gently rolling Nene Valley. It sat at the southern edge of town

and guarded the borders of his world. Beyond, there were just open
fields and the odd village explored by bicycle – Shutlanger, Milton
Malsor, Stoke Bruene, Blisworth – all the way to the M1.

He passed the stacks of concrete leftover from the building of
the bypass that were known to them as Stonehenge … that strange
place he had seen featured on Arthur C. Clarke's *Mysterious World*.
His mum had bought him a copy of the book for Christmas and
he had poured over its many wonders.

The sunlight blinked at him through the canopy of trees. He did a
circuit of the hillfort ramparts – a maze of dips and hollows now covered in oak and ash – popular with the BMX brigade, but for now
he had it to himself. It was Saturday, and while many of his school
friends would be in town, he had chosen the freedom of Hunsbury.

The boy was a bit of a daydreamer and loner. He found it easier
to be in his own company. The funny thing was he never felt alone
in nature. His head was filled with stories, conjured up by the trees,
bumps and hollows of his neck of the woods. A funny phrase … if a
wood had a neck, then surely, it followed, it must have a head, shoulders, belly, bum and feet? And a heart. He had yearned to find the
heart of the woods, but it was well hidden. Every copse of trees had
one, even the spindly spinneys near where he lived, which had been
nibbled away by farming and the tamed greens of the golf course.
There was one tree that contained the wood's heart and he was yet to
find it in Hunsbury, but not through want of looking.

He had found many other things in the process of his search:
odd-shaped stones that might have been old arrow heads (or 'elf-
shot'); a Roman coin; curiously shaped bottles from yesteryear;
and his greatest treasure, a bronze brooch – weathered, but when
rubbed up, showing a glimmer of its former glory. Sometimes he
would bring one of his hoard out with him on his adventures and
in a secret place, hidden away from prying eyes and sticky fingers,
he would sit with it and it would whisper to him.

His most curious finds were bits of what looked like blackened
glass. They were scattered all across the old earthworks, often dug
up by the badgers and rabbits that made a swiss-cheese of the
ancient defences – ramparts that must have once stood tall and

proud, with a palisade of sharpened timbers, patrolled by spiky haired warriors protecting the tribe inside. Copying the books in the school library, he had done drawings of the 'hill people', as he called them, giving them names and imagining their lives in exhaustive detail.

That day, as he was sitting in his favourite spot – the crook of an old oak – he heard the chilling noise of Filchy and his gang, cursing and cracking their way through the undergrowth. A knot of fear gripped his stomach. If they caught him they would nick his bike, or worse, his treasure: for that day he had brought the bronze brooch with him. He might be able to avoid detection in the tree, but his Chopper bike, leaning below, would not. Then they would find him! It didn't bear thinking about.

Heart beating wildly, he leapt down and jumped on his bike, cycling like a mad thing away from the approaching thugs, the bane of his school life. Even on the estate it wasn't safe to be out when they were abroad. 'Hey!' a shout went up. 'It's that little weasel. Oi! Billy No Mates, come back 'ere!'

They had spotted him – he pumped the pedals as fast as he could. Maybe if he made it to the 'Grand Canyon' – as everyone called the ironstone quarry – he would be able to make it across to safety. There was a metal pole going across, and it was possible to hitch over to the other side, hanging by one's arms over the twenty-foot drop. Scary, but he had done it before, egged on by his friends. This time he had no choice. He would have to hide his bike and make a break for it – hoping they wouldn't find it, or cross before he had legged it.

Hurtling down the track, he cast frantically about for a hiding place. The gravel path was lined by abandoned vehicles – broken windscreens, flat tyres, chassis rusting red. How they had ended up here, he didn't know. It was like an elephant's graveyard for cars. Some were clearly the result of joyriders; but others looked too old and dilapidated: jalopies from another era.

Round the back of one he could stow his bike. There was a thicket – hard, but not impossible to get into if you wriggled low. He would slide his bike in there and hope for the best.

He coasted to a stop by the wreck – an old lorry with its bonnet up, from which grew young ash saplings. He pulled the bike around the back and slid it under the trees. Just then he heard the borish voices of the gang. They had run after him. He had no chance of making the canyon now. He hid in the shadows, eyes peering out as they swaggered nearby, banging on the rusting metal with sticks: 'Where is the little toe rag?'

The boy shuffled as silently as he could backwards into the undergrowth, covered his bike with mulch, and prayed he wouldn't be seen. He bumped into something hard, and looking behind him he saw a thick ash with a hollow trunk. It was an old, old tree. He crawled inside and crouched down low, holding his breath. He held the brooch in his sweating fist, kissing it for luck, eyes squeezed shut.

Don't let them see me, don't let them see … Make me invisible.

Suddenly, the world seemed to turn inside out. The boy gasped and opened his eyes. And flinched. The undergrowth that had been concealing him now seemed like … glass. He reached out a shaking hand. His hand struck a branch. The tree was still there, hard but transparent.

Then, a feeling of dread came over him – they will be able to see him!

Nervously looking beyond the thicket, a strange sight presented itself to him. Not only was the old truck transparent, but also the figures of the gang. He could see them, just – the light bending around them as they flailed about jokingly.

The boy wriggled out of his hole and stood up … they didn't seem to notice him, although, looking down at his body, he seemed solid enough.

Then, a strange thought occurred to him.

Perhaps they hadn't become invisible … maybe he had! He looked at the brooch in his hand, which looked real and old. He held it tight, feeling reassured by its cool presence, and walked easily between the boys. David McCallum, eat your heart out!

He couldn't resist giving Filchy a pinch on the ear as he passed.

'Oi! What the – ? Right, which one of you wallies did that?' He turned on his gang and starting pushing them around. Leaving them to squabble, the boy slipped away, towards the earthworks. From a distance they seemed solid, but the closer he got the more they seemed to melt away. As he scrambled up the earthen bank, it felt as though he was standing on a glass hill, an unnerving feeling. It wasn't slippy, the ground still felt like soil, but the sensation was vertigo-inducing and made him feel slightly nauseous. It was hard to see where he was treading. He tried to test each footing first, but inevitably he tripped and found himself tumbling down the bank. Determined to hold onto the brooch, he wasn't able to stop his fall easily, and ended up banging his head as he collided with a tree – suddenly very real and present.

When the stars cleared, he looked around him and gasped.

Before him stood a village of roundhouses with thatched roofs and simple doorways of heavy material. Smoke curled from them, seeping through the thatch. Somewhere a blacksmith's hammer clinked on an anvil; a horse whinnied – short and stocky, with a thick mane – a group of raggedy children ran past, laughing. The people were dressed in simple tunics, coloured with natural dyes. The men's hair was spiked and limed; the women's braided and ornamented with pins. Arms were bare and bulged with spiralling tattoos and metalwork. Warriors swaggered about with swords and spears. A group were returning now, carrying a deer lashed to a long pole over their shoulders, followed by hunting dogs. Hens clucked and pecked amid the huts, and a tethered goat bleated.

Everything seemed so real.

But when he looked down at himself, he realised he now was 'glass'. His hand still felt solid, and still held the brooch – opaque and gleaming in the sunlight – but he was now see-through. A weird sensation, although he took some delight in it at being the invisible boy!

He walked among the hill fort settlement, thrilled at seeing this Iron Age world brought so vividly to life. It was just as he had imagined, but more so. He loved noticing the little details – the sheer texture of it all – more than any book or museum could realise.

'Who are you?'

The boy jumped. A woman with long prematurely grey hair was looking at him – the cool blue of her eyes looking straight at him.

He turned and looked behind him. There was no one else nearby.

She jabbed a long fingernail at him. 'Yes, you boy!'

The woman circled him, inspecting him, testing if he was there or not – brazenly probing and muttering away.

'Don't think I can't see you, I can – Old Meghannuith has the sight, whatever they say.' She scrutinised his appearance. 'But … you are not like the others.'

She grabbed the brooch. Before the boy could react, she was holding it firmly in her hand – as though she had plucked it out of the air. 'Where did you get this?' She turned it over, inspecting it, rubbing it on the hem of her skirts. 'Are you a thief?'

The boy started to whimper. Hot tears welled up in his eyes.

'No. You haven't got the balls. Not yet,' she snorted. 'You found it somewhere then. Curious …' For a moment she contemplated the clouds carefully, apparently noticing certain qualities which satisfied her. 'Come with me.'

She started to walk off.

'Wait, without it I can't get back …'

'What was that? Home, you say … ? Where is home, eh? It looks like you've come a long way. I bet you're hungry.'

The boy's stomach grumbled. He nodded, shyly.

'I've got something to put flesh on a ghost. You have to trust me.'

She led on.

Meg (as he thought of her, unable to pronounce her name properly) opened up the flap of her roundhouse on the edge of the enclosure. 'Come on in then, before folk think I've turned fey – talking to thin air. I give them enough to yabber about as it is.'

The boy nervously entered the dark hut, at least that's how it seemed at first, but as his eyes adjusted he noted the details – herbs hanging to dry, pots and pans, phials of potions, a raven's wing, the skull of a deer, two cats – one pure black, one pure white slinking around her legs before settling back by the fire, which seemed to spring into life as Meg whispered at it.

'Sit yourself down – over there. Don't touch anything.'

Clumsily, he stepped over the clutter and made his way to the clear corner, a little wooden stool by the firepit, where a pot bubbled away. Meg sang tunelessly to herself as she plucked off herbs to throw in and stir.

'There.' She ladled some of the pale, watery broth in a bowl and handled it to him. 'Get it down you, it won't hurt. It's spirit broth.' She cackled. 'Should put some meat on your bones.'

The boy sniffed it gingerly. It smelled of old boots.

'Go on! It won't kill you.'

Reluctantly he took a sip – it tasted better than it looked. In truth, he was feeling chilled. The whole experience had been overwhelming. The shock had left him numb at first, but now it was setting in and he found himself shaking.

'Here.' She threw a blanket next to him.

He wrapped it around his shoulders and carried on sipping – gazing into the flames.

Meg talked at him for what seemed an age, until all her words blurred into one. The boy felt sleepy – the fire, the warmth, the shock of it all – now made him yawn, and he found himself nodding off.

When he awoke, he was outside of the earthworks, lying on the ground next to the ash tree by his bike. Everything looked normal again. For a moment he panicked, but he still held the brooch lightly in his grasp. Carefully putting it away, he wriggled out, pulling the Chopper behind him. He got up and brushed the leaves off, catching his breath.

Suddenly, he was startled by a bark. Turning, he saw a man was walking his dog. Approaching, the walker looked a bit concerned. 'Are you alright son?'

The boy mumbled, 'Okay.' He got on his bike and quickly cycled away.

Before entering the 'time tunnel' he looked back at the hill fort – its trees silhouetted against the setting sun. It looked solid enough. What had he experienced? A dream? His head hurt, that's for sure. His fingers inspected a light graze there from where he bumped it. Pulling his hood up, he headed home. It was getting dark and the lamp posts were winking on, yellow eyes watching him all the way down Towcester Road.

The boy thought about his strange adventure through the whole of the next week – hardly paying attention to any of the lessons, the dictates of the teachers, the derision of the pupils. It all seemed to fade into the background. He kept the brooch in his pocket – it was his touchstone. It, at least, felt real.

As soon as he could he returned to Hunsbury Hill, nervous that somehow it wouldn't be there. But there it stood on the skyline – at the top of the Towcester Road, a steep slog on the bike. Past the cemetery, and through the 'time tunnel' and he was back. He rode quickly up the gravel path to the earthworks – into the middle of them, through a gap. Throwing down his bike, he pulled out the brooch and gave it a rub. 'Make me invisible like David McCallum!' he said under his breath, closing his eyes. Nothing. He looked around and everything was still normal. It didn't work. Then he remembered.

The heart of the wood! The Grandmother Ash – he raced over to it and squeezed through the gap into the thicket. There it was, dark and silent. He sat in its hollow trunk and tried again.

'McCallum! McCallum!' he chanted. This time the brooch's magic did the trick.

The woodland melted away around him. Excited, he made his way to the glass fort. As he slid down the other side, the village of roundhouses appeared. He made his way to Meg's hut and pulled back the flap.

'So you're back then, are you?'

Meg didn't seem surprised.

This time the boy was alert and listened closely as the old woman asked him question after question about where he came from and what it was like. She listened in grim silence.

And then she shared her own story.

'I have always had the sight – since I was a stripling I saw things. The Others. The People of Peace. Spirits of Place. I kept myself to myself, preferring my own company. I was shunned. Feared a little, even. My mother had taught me the names and properties of the plants, but she didn't have the "gift" like I – though sometimes it felt more like a curse. Apparently, my grandmother had the Sight, but she died when I was still very young. My mother warned me to keep my secret to myself, although folk came to our door often enough wanting a cure for this or that. It was the Druids' business to commune with the ancestors and whatnot. We could not be seen subverting their authority. Otherwise, what use would their robes and staves and fancy language be? So I kept to my simple hedge-witchery, always kneeling amid the undergrowth looking for this or that. Oh, how my poor old knees ache now! My mother died, though I was able to ease her passing; but I have no one to pass my lore onto now. The menfolk have shunned me. Some find me ugly. I mind not. I have my cats, and my potions, and the Others.'

It was getting dark by the time she finished. The woman sat in the gloom of the hut, and the boy imagined her there by herself. It felt sad. He sensed her loneliness, but when he reached out she brushed him away.

'I'm busy now. Skat.' She started clattering about with her pestle and mortar.

'Can I come back?' the boy asked.

The woman didn't look up. But she said, casually, as though it mattered not, 'If you want.'

As the boy left, one of the Druids stared across at Meg's hut.

The boy returned as often as he could. It was half-term and he went every day, delighted to hear Meg's stories – wild and magical tales that lingered in the air. She shared fragments of wisdom – 'rags and tatters', as she put it – of folklore, herblore, and song.

Then one day the boy returned and immediately sensed something was wrong. The sky looked angry and there was unrest in the air. To his horror he saw a column of smoke rising from Meg's hut. It was on fire! He scanned about urgently and saw that she was being driven out of the hill fort by angry and frightened tribes people, carrying torches. Her hands were tied behind her back.

The Druids were casting her out.

'Meghannuith, you have been spotted speaking to the Others without the intervention of the priesthood. You have refused to undertake training in the necessary degree. You would have made a fine Ovate, but haughtily you have rejected this path. Despite several warnings you have persisted in your hag craft. We cannot have anyone dabbling in the realms of Spirit. The cosmos is a delicate and intricate mechanism – not to be left to amateurs to tinker with. You are cast out of the village, and taken to the neighbouring tun – there you will judged as they see fit.'

Her eyes flared with anger as a heavy lead collar was placed around her neck. She was lifted into a cart pulled by oxen.

As she was led through the large wooden gates marking the Western exit, she turned, wild-haired and called out, cursing them – her voice high and strangled in the collar.

A wild wind whipped up, snatching torches from hands and setting the palisade alight. The flames spread quicker than they could be put out.

The Druids tried to restore order and bellowed out orders, but the panic spread like the enchanted flames, which seemed to possess a sinister intelligence. Soon the whole hill fort was encircled in a ring of fire. The villagers huddled in the centre, helpless as the blaze consumed their defences.

Meg laughed from her cart, which was suddenly jerked away as the terrified oxen bolted.

'Run, boy! Run!' she called out – her voice carrying across the roar of the flames into his mind. It yanked him like a thread into action. He found himself running, running towards the dwindling gap. There was one section that had not caught fire yet.

Heart bursting in the heat, he dashed towards it, knocking a Druid flying. 'The witch's demon! Stop him!'

Villagers were too preoccupied with saving themselves and their belongings, and the Druid went unheeded.

Gasping for air, the boy made his way through the last gap – before the wall of flame cut him off from the village.

He scrambled down the henge and up the other side to safety, the mulch cool beneath him, the heat of the blaze on his skin. He held his brooch tightly in his trembling fist.

When he finally was able to return – several days later, clutching the brooch – he was unable to 'cross over'. He wandered the earthworks, gazing forlornly into the enclosure, which stubbornly remained empty of all signs of life. He kicked the soil in frustration, dislodging a piece of what looked like blackened glass. He picked it up and held it to the light, thinking of Meg. He hoped she had been alright. He returned to the ash tree and buried his brooch there in her memory – asking Grandmother Ash to keep her from harm. Although he knew she must have lived centuries ago and would be nothing but dust by now, another part of him believed she still lived on somewhere, somehow. All periods of history co-existing … he struggled to find an analogy. He looked at the black glass and a flash of inspiration came to him. If he had managed to crossover once, he could do it again … even if it took him the rest of his life.

'I'll visit you again. I'll find you. I promise.'

The old ash tree sighed in the winds. Ash keys fell around him, as the branches let them go.

The wise woman had taught him so much. He vowed never to forget her stories, her lore. 'Thank you Meg.'

Pocketing the piece of glass, he turned and cycled through the trees.

I grew up playing over Hunsbury Hill (or Danes Camp as it was also known). It was an adventure playground, tinged with an atmosphere of old magic. Situated between my school and my grandparents' house in Briar Hill (home to a Roman villa and evidence of settlement reaching back to 3500 BC), it provided a welcome refuge from the mundanity of estate life and the brutish horrors of a comprehensive school. It is now a country park, ringed in by estates and, apparently, gangs of thieves. In the 1960s, a druid

group used it when access to Stonehenge was denied. As a young adult I organised an Earth Rhythm Camp there – to have a taste of tribal life.

Around 400 BC there is evidence of a defensive settlement at Hunsbury Hill. The site was occupied for the next 400 years. In the late 1990s, the remains of a thirty to forty-year-old woman from the former Iron Age village of Great Houghton was discovered. The skeleton, when carbon dated, was discovered to be 2,400 years old. She wore an unusual heavy lead 'torc' collar around her neck – that, and her position (crouched, with her hands tied behind her back) suggested she might have been buried alive: 'The only answer which fits the facts is that she was a Celtic witch, buried weighted down to keep her from moving.' (Andrew Selkirk, editor of Current Archaeology).

In this story I combine the archaeological evidence of Hunsbury Hill (its vitrified earthworks unusual in England) and the woman of Great Houghton (contemporary to the site's construction), with my childhood memories of the place, the names associated with it in my neighbourhood amongst the boys of my age, and my imagination. For many of us growing up in the estates of Far Cotton, Delapré and Briar Hill it was a tantalising portal to another time – a tangible reminder of our prehistoric past. This story has been pieced together from these fragments – archaeological fact, local history, childhood memory, and imagination – 'the rags and tatters' that all went into my folk-tale cauldron. It was important to get the blend right, the optimum mix of accuracy and artistic license. Sometimes I had to add my own 'flavourings' to up the ante. Celtic Iron Age society had three castes – Bard, Ovate and Druid. They would probably have been more tolerant to those who had the 'Sight', but for the purposes of the story I increased their antagonism for dramatic effect (as a rationale for explaining the 'witch's' exile and burial). Certainly, those who follow modern day Druidry are far more open-minded, and many witches have become druids, or work closely with them, yet the mystery of the Great Houghton burial remains.

THREE

THE LEGEND
OF RAGENER

In the time of Edward the Confessor, in the small town of Hamtun, the church of St Peter's was raised by Simon de Senlis on the site of an older Saxon one – a clear power statement by the Norman invaders: a mailed gauntlet fist, pounding down the oppressed.

Yet, the spirit of the people is like a sleeping giant, and though dormant for many years, can rise up again. Sometimes, the true treasure is hiding in plain sight – overlooked by the haughty overlords, who saw little of value in the Saxon settlement overlooking the Nene beyond the sweat of their slaves.

There was a wealthy priest named Bruningus who was Rector of Saint Peter's Church, among others, and he had a young servant of Norwegian descent, as his straw-blonde hair and sea-blue eyes testified. This servant was said to be of remarkable simplicity; his pure heart devoted to the worship of his Drotinum – his lord – Saint Peter.

One day, he was possessed with the idea of journeying to Rome, on a Holy Pilgrimage, to seek his Drotinum. He asked permission from his master to go, but he was invaluable to Bruningus; he could not relieve him of his duties, yet his refusal was chiefly because of his great fondness for the lad – he did not want to see him go because he knew that the servant would have trouble looking after himself in the big wide world, for he was reputed to be a fool by all who knew him … but then the wisest often are.

The servant could not take no for an answer and repeated his request as though his very existence relied upon it. His friends thought it only a strange whim, but he had never been more serious in his life. Finally, Bruningus, getting no peace from the boy, relented and his servant set off urgently. After a few days on the road, the young Norwegian rested, footsore and somewhat frightened. He had never travelled alone before and he was in unknown territory. He lit a small fire and, taking a few of his rations, tried to get some sleep. Alas, every sinister sound in the forest prevented him from doing so. Then, just as he accepted whatever fate had in store for him and his lids grew heavy, all went deathly quiet and – Lo! – a ghostly vision appeared to him of a venerable looking man who bade him to return home at great speed, for he will find his Lord there. Furthermore, that if he continued his foolish venture then his life would be in danger.

Terrified but resolute, he continued on, taking the apparition to be but a nightmare, the Devil leading him astray. He resumed his journey, rattled but determined to not be thwarted from his goal, until the same unnatural encounter occurred again that very next night, with the phantom even more insistent that he turn back.

Unnerved to say the least, the young pilgrim hardened himself against these ill-omens and carried on stubbornly. As the fatigue of his trek overcame him more and more each night, sleep came mercifully easier to him. However, a Holy Messenger cannot be ignored for long and even the realms of sleep offered no sanctuary from his persistent spirit: it manifested once again, whilst the seeker slumbered and gave him no respite – it was most wrathful at his ignorance and tormented him all night. The servant needed no further persuasion and headed back at first light.

His premature return was met with derision; so much for his oh-so important pilgrimage! The scornful voices were silenced though when they heard of his visions. He was too dull to make up such a tale. Bruningus was so touched by his tribulations and true heart that he set him free from his service so that he could pursue whatever divine course that was allotted him. The servant boy, now a free man, used his liberty wisely by praying and fasting, in the hope that his vision's message and what his Lord had shown him would come true.

A year and a half passed in which he devoted himself to his new master – the Almighty – before his prayers were finally answered. The Celestial Being materialised before him one evening whilst he rested after his worship – it was the same venerable figure, with his flowing silvery beard. This time he smiled benignly at his disciple and beckoned him to rise and follow, to where his desires shall be fulfilled. As his body slept, his soul was guided to a corner of the ancient church where, the phantom told him, the 'chosen friend of God lay'. He was instructed to tell the priest, Bruningus, for he will know what to do. This the young monk did, for he too was a man of God; thus, in the morning the Rector was informed and, after deliberating upon the Holy Vision, the priest took a spade and dug at the spot indicated by the phantom and now the monk, when suddenly the tool struck stone!

Bruningus frantically excavated the mass of soil before carefully scraping away the remaining earth with the monk's help and, lo and behold, a fantastic tomb was revealed! It depicted, in ornate Saxon style, a bearded man entwined within the tree of life, with a bestiary of fabulous beasts around him. It was surely the resting place of some important personage, Bruningus presumed, but who? He hesitated at desecrating the tomb, although he and the monk were both greatly intrigued as to whom it contained. While they meditated upon what to do, the discovery was announced and townsfolk flocked to see it.

It amazed all who saw it, yet no one, not even the town elders, knew who it was for. The tomb was placed there before living memory and concealed for what purpose? Finally, Bruningus devised a scheme whereby the identity of the sarcophagus' occupant could be revealed and not by one of the nobility, who may benefit from 'discovering the honoured ancestor to be his own', but by one of lowly birth who would have nothing to lose in divining the truth.

So, that Easter, Bruningus came across an unfortunate cripple, crawling across the market square – it was Alfgiva, a native woman of Abington, whose hamstrings had contracted at birth. She was often seen begging upon her hands and knees, for that was all she could walk upon. The priest asked her if she would like to be cured. Of course she would, but how? Nothing short of a miracle would suffice. 'Do the Lord's bidding,' Bruningus spoke, 'and your afflictions may be lifted.' It is well known that those with shrivelled bodies or minds have been touched by God. Some said Alfgiva had the sight also. She was ideal.

Seeing that things may work to her advantage, Alfgiva agreed and the priest told her what she must do. On the night of Christ's resurrection, she was to purify herself and, after her confession, to spend an evening in ardent prayer, keeping vigil over the tomb in hope of a sign.

So, Alfgiva was left, huddled next to the candle-lit lid, upon which her faery eyes were fixed, beads in hand and incantations on her lips, as the priest locked her in for the night. Alone at last, she relaxed into earnest contemplation. The priests made her nervous with all their strange demands and requests but now she could concentrate upon her task. She prayed, not for healing, because miracles never occur on demand, but for insight, a glimpse of the truth. Who did the slab conceal? The uncanny patterns seemed to come alive as she stared at them … the two dragons, biting their own tails … a regal lion in a circular seal … a goat nurturing its kid … the blossoming tree with its swirling interlocking branches … a bird whispering into the backward ears of the man's head, foliage disgorging from his open mouth? But, distantly wondered Alfgiva, why is he upside down to everything else and where is his body?

The answers seemed to be locked within her own pounding skull and, just as the solution to the slab's riddle began to present itself to her, the church filled with celestial splendour, dazzling Algiva. She gasped and covered her eyes; then, daring to peep through her trembling fingers, she saw a snow-white dove appear out of the divine radiance and swoop about the church. It plunged into the font as though possessed with a purpose and, soaring baptised from here, sprayed Alfgiva and the tomb with the Holy Water from its wing tips. Then – glory be told! – the cowering cripple rose miraculously to her full height, cured of her terrible curse! The wonders did not cease there: two bells that hung a distance apart in the tower began to chime in harmonious union, as if rung by the hands of an expert puller!

Bruningus and his clerks heard this joyous peel, as did most of Hamtun, and it startled them all, for the sound was uncommon at such a late hour. One by one they awoke and came running up to the blessed chapel, sleepy but excited. They blinked at the majestic glow issuing from the stained-glass windows, the rainbow colours of the saints painting their awestruck faces. The church seemed ablaze with its own sun.

Summoning courage, a few of them approached the door and unbarred it, whereupon the magnificent spectacle was displayed to them: Alfgiva, standing upright for the first time in her life, her tattered dress rising above her knees now too short for her long, straight legs.

Others crowded the church now and many fell down in genuflection before the miracle, weeping in joy and terror. Those not struck dumb stuttered prayers to their Lord, whose power was so wondrously manifested before them. The music and light made them reel but it eventually faded and Alfgiva sat weakly down, somewhat stunned. When they had all calmed down, Bruningus and the monk enquired what happened, and she told them as well as she could.

The priest was now certain that the tomb contained someone of real majesty, although Alfgiva had not been told his identity. Bruningus still hesitated before breaking the tomb seal, for he did not know if he was worthy of the deed, or if anyone was. Yet, as news of that night's events spread like wildfire, he set to praying and fasting for three days to test his mettle. Finally, he felt he was ready – he had been 'told' that the task had to be his and so, weak and wild-eyed, he made his way to the tomb with the appropriate tools, accompanied by his clerks and a whole host of the infirm, aged and blighted who had heard of the miracle church where they may be cured too.

Without ceremony, the near delirious Bruningus set to opening the tomb, jemmying back the lid. As the seal was broken, the last breath of the expired hissed out. Such was the holiness of the man interred that all those present were filled with his divine goodness and cured, all at once, of any affliction, no matter how tiny or terrible.

The coffin lid was lifted away by the monk and clerks, though it weighed massively, and within the mortal remains of a true martyr were exposed, as stated by the inscription therein which read: 'Here lieth Ragener, holy martyr of Christ and nephew of Saint Edmund, King, cruelly slain by the Danes, AD 870.'

Beholding this marvel the multitude let out a tremendous cheer, for laying before them was the ancient King of Hamtun himself, as whispered in fireside legends, who would one day be reborn to save the town in its darkest hour (his name meaning 'born of the people's strength', as Bruningus brethlessly explained).

As the afflicted were healed, so would be the town. Reports of the incredible events travelled far and soon hordes of pilgrims descended upon the town to see the martyr's remains. Oblations accumulated about the open tomb, as rich and poor alike left some token of their own esteem. Hearing of this, Edward visited the church in person and seeing the diverse and dazzling riches, both secular and spiritual, therein bestowed, he ordered a shrine to be built to accommodate it all, for every day more gift-laden pilgrims arrived from far and wide and from that year on not just the wealthy, but the weak, sick and dying congregated upon the shrine during the Feast of the Apostles, Saint Peter and Saint Paul, in the hope of being blessed or cured.

The Norwegian monk initiated the Fraternity of Ruginary, devoted to the memory and care of the Martyr. The members, many of them the clerks of the church, dedicated themselves to the protection of the shrine, defending it against Hamtun's enemies.

What became of Algiva? She grew to be a strong and famous woman, taking the habit, and leading a virtuous life. Such was her reputation for sanctity that she was commonly known as the Holy Nun.

The Norwegian became quite a celebrity in the years following the visions, impressing even the invaders with his humility and devotion. He was commanded to recount his experience to their courts, which was a rare but dubious experience for an outsider.

And so, thanks to this nameless Northman, the legend of Ragener was discovered and preserved. While the martyr's memory lives on, the spirit of Hamtun will not die, for it is born of the people's strength.

I originally researched and wrote this for my first attempt at a novel, The Ghost Tree, *back in 1992–5. The tomb lid of Ragener can still be seen in the back of St Peter's – which is worth visiting for the corbel stones alone, which adorn its outside eaves. It is a rare fragment of old Hamtun – the original settlement of Northampton. A Great Hall is said to have been constructed next to St Peter's Church in Marefair between Gold Street and the Railway Station. Evidence of this was uncovered by archaeologists during the 1990s redevelopment of what is now called 'Saxon Rise'. This was reputed to be the home of a prince and was originally constructed of timber around AD 750 and was rebuilt from stone and made much larger seventy years later.*

FOUR

THE GREAT FIRE OF NORTHAMPTON

Nine years after the Great Fire of London, Northampton had its own conflagration. For those who saw it, it was said to be twice as bad. They both happened in the same month – September – and after a dry summer, the densely populated settlements of dwellings made of wood and thatched roofs, packed into narrow lanes, were like tinder-boxes.

On the twentieth of that month, something or someone sparked it off, and for those who witnessed it, that day would be branded into their memory.

It was half past the eleventh hour when it started. Bright but blustery and, oh, what an ill wind blew that day, as the hands of the clock of All Hallows' Church edged towards noon.

The common opinion, which is seldom right, has it that the fire was caused by the 'carelessness of an infamous woman' … perhaps merely a single mother forced to go out for a minute – her hearth fire dwindling as she was simmering some broth for her and her littl' un. Maybe she nipped next door to get a shovelful of faggots from a kind neighbour and got caught up in a bit of gossip: a moment's distraction in the daily grind. It could have been any reason – understandable, perfectly human, and perfectly fallible. A door left ajar; a sudden gust of wind; luck; chance; carelessness; or fate – who knows? Who can say? Perhaps the 'infamous woman' tripped, scattering the hot embers into a ramshackle pile of kindling and it quickly combusted. A falling timber might have blocked off access to a bucket of water, even blocked the way out. Was she trapped inside? Or did she escape, clutching her bab to her breast?

The fire certainly did. It leapt from house to house, catching easily on the parched thatch. Squeezed together in their poverty, the dwellings – leaning precariously close to one another – ignited and the whole cursed street was ablaze in no time at all.

Alas, the flames didn't stop there. Animated by a harsh west wind, the hungry tongues darted amongst ricks of corn and maltings on Horsemarket, and soon the cry of 'Fire! Fire!' was heard abroad, though some fools made light of it, believing it to be far off and affecting meaner dwellings than their own. Others hoped it would spend itself out in the large cherry orchard next to the castle remains.

How wrong they all were.

The bell of All Hallows was rung for the last time that noontide – and it tolled doom for the town.

The westerly wind, which blew the flames swifter than horsed men, had carried its fiery riders all the way along Swineshead to the Dern Gate; at least half a mile from the place it began its deadly life.

And it didn't stop there. It continued to within spitting distance of St Giles' Church, combusting every house along that fair street.

In such a situation, folk start to get plain foolish, trying to save their precious belongings, even if they have to risk life and limb to do so. Chaos ensued. The heat and smoke was intense. It was as though the very pits of Hell had opened up; folk were knocking one another aside, desperate to save their cherished treasures, heirlooms and families; but others had begun working together to combat the disaster – gentlemen and labourers alike relayed buckets to quench the insatiable blaze. However, their valiant efforts were in vain; as were the attempts to create a gap that would check the flames, by blasting unsalvageable habitations in its path with the remaining powderkegs – what hadn't already exploded amongst the barrels that had been recently unloaded in the streets, but not yet stored or sold.

Whatever attempts were made to stem the terror, nothing could check the baleful pyre – it sucked in everything in its way. Within three hours the town was being so ravaged that only a damn good downpour could have stopped it.

Yet God, if the Almighty was watching, wept no tears for Northampton that day. Nor had he for some time, it seemed, for it had been a dry summer and what added to the volatile situation and made it even more devastating were the freshly-delivered supplies for winter, filling the provision stores.

A perfect firestorm.

The flames, passing over the grounds of St Katherine's, seized upon College land, finding there great quantities of oil and tallow and other combustible material: this gave it enough strength to break through the back of the Drapery in but a brief gust – a fireball sending the Snippers scattering.

When it reached Wood Hill, turning the corner towards the Town Hall, a terrible sight greeted onlookers – the Church of All Hallows itself was ablaze! Not even God's house could escape this scathing avenger.

The church, still the largest and most central in the town after being rebuilt, was then twice the size – extending as far west as east.

At its fulcrum rose the great bell tower, which now served a different function, as a chimney – the flames and smoke being sucked up into it from all sides. It belched forth the ashes of the town like a volcanic kraken. And with one gulp, the ancient bell, which had tolled for townsmen and king alike, was sent crashing into the beast's cindery bowels with a deafening clang – the last sound it ever made, chiming Hamtun's doom.

In Market Hill, desperate citizens piled their goods, hoping that their possessions would be safe in the square, the widest in England. Yet if the temple place offered no respite, what chance had the traders, in theirs?

It was the very picture of the end of the world – as frantic men and women scoured the crowd for their loved ones, all faces blurred into one expression of terror. The square was surrounded by flames. The townsfolk had been so busy stacking their goods, that none had noticed the fire close in upon them.

The heat pressed in and it seemed like they were in Hell itself. That infernal temperature alone caused the market cross to ignite, and it raged before them all – a sign of their damnation, it seemed. The pump's water began to boil over and they could not use it anymore. The end was surely nigh and perhaps a good thing too, according to the zealots, for the town had grown corrupt. They had brought it upon us, the wild-eyed fanatics ranted.

Then, at this eleventh hour, salvation was offered.

In the corner of the square, one house still stood amongst the tumbling rows – for it was made of stone.

Danver's house.

The crowds all but stampeded towards it.

Mercifully, they were saved.

Though the Fire devastated the town, it claimed only eight souls. Two men were found under a collapsed chimney in St Mary's Street. Over six hundred houses were lost – homes to seven hundred families. Thousands and thousands of pounds caused in damage, in ruined businesses. And even those who had managed to salvage some of their worldly goods found them stolen the next morning by heartless thieves.

What a dismal scene it was that confronted the townsfolk the next day: a town of ghosts, filled with the smoky phantoms of folks' lives and livelihoods. It was like the aftermath of a great battle. Blackened survivors wandered around in a daze. Some scavenged for a blanket; a crust of bread; or simply sat, bent in silence, by the roadside. Occasionally, a grief-stricken individual would be seen frantically scouring the remains for someone or thing of value to them. An ashen infant would scream for its mother, a parent for their child.

Yet amongst the tragedies there were glimpses of hope. A family would weep with joy, reunited; the humble and great alike gave what they could. For a while there was little distinction between rich and poor as folk shared what they had. Those fortunate enough to have their homes intact took in those that were not. It took the town's darkest hour to bring its populace together.

The news of the catastrophe spread as fast as the smoke which alerted people from miles around, including Hamtun's Earl himself. He dutifully summoned help from further afield and sent in supplies. With his aid, and others, the disaster was slowly dealt with; its victims picking up the pieces of their lives it had left them.

A meeting was held the following Sunday in the Town Hall, which still stood, squat and square, next to the market square, along with Danver's place, Hazelrigg House and the four cardinal churches: St Giles in the east, St Sep's in the north, St Peter's in the west, and St John's Hospice in the south. Of the rest of the town – its stores, inns and slums – little else remained.

At the meeting, the nobility and gentlemen of the county set about the task of raising funds to help rebuild old Hamtun. Aid was being received from far and wide to help the townsfolk rebuild their own lives – from Cambridge, Oxford, London, including from the King himself. With the generosity of his 'Divine Grace', King Charles II, the town was rebuilt with a thousand tonnes of timber from the Royal Forests of Whittlewood and Salcey. He had once hid in an oak tree, and that had saved his hide. Now the trees were saving the town's.

In remembrance, the grateful townsfolk place an oak garland on the Merry Monarch's statue above the portico of All Hallows every Oak Apple Day – like good subjects of the Crown. Northampton had reached for the fire of the gods – when the Civil War threatened to set the country alight – and had been duly punished. The castle had been pulled down, but perhaps that hadn't been enough to teach this stubborn shoe-town a lesson.

What had been the true cause of the Great Fire?

There were strange murmurings. A man had been seen running up Gold Street with a keg of gunpowder under his arm. Not the sort of thing one would choose to do in the middle of a blaze, unless you wanted to die – or were being paid lots of money. Had old Charley wanted revenge on what had been a Cromwellian stronghold? The maker of Roundhead boots? With our leather on their feet, they had marched to war.

But folk forget. They move on. Hamtun wanted to put the dark past behind it; begin afresh. As clean wide streets emerged and the filthy narrow back alleys disappeared so too did their bad dreams. There was much to occupy them. The ancient street plan was kept – just like on John Speed's map – though roads were widened, new stone constructions like the Sessions House erected; trade increased, bringing prosperity back to the town – which rose phoenix-like from the ashes.

The Great Fire of Northampton was devastating and transformed the look of the town as it was rebuilt, with a more widely spaced street plan. The whole affair seems almost biblical … and the evidence suggests it might have indeed been an act of judgement, but whose?

FIVE

THE
LAST WITCHES

It was a Saturday, 17 March 1705. Two women in chains were carted to meet their fate at Gallows' Corner, on the edge of the Racecourse – just north of Northampton. There was a wildness in the air, whipping the still bare branches into life, reflecting the mood of the crowd which converged on the fateful corner, a humming mass, greedy for spectacle, driven by fear and bloodlust. An execution was a good distraction from the daily grind, but today was special. Today, two notorious witches were going to swing.

Swing and burn.

Mary Shaw and Elinor Philips were taken in a cart to their final destination. The crowds were desperate to catch a glimpse of them, at the same time as crossing themselves in fear. Some even clutched 'charms' to ward of their evil eye. 'Look at them! Look at the witches!'

The doomed pair should have made a pitiful sight – shaven heads, threadbare and filfthy smocks, sunken cheeked and hollow-eyed from who knows what unspeakable cruelty, and yet they stood defiantly, holding each other for support, fending off the scraps and insults thrown at them with dignity.

Some said they appeared so calm because they had boasted that their master would not suffer them to be executed and that he would save them at the eleventh hour.

He did not seem forthcoming on that day.

The day before they had been put on trial at the assizes, and found guilty of witchcraft after several testimonies were heard against them and their 'confessions' read out, which detailed their notorious careers in lascivious detail. Many elements of the trial were shared and discussed like good juicy gossip amongst the populace – it spiced up a dull morning no end. Yet all wanted to hear it from the horse's mouth. They wanted to be able to tell their grandchildren that 'they had been there' the day 'two of the most notorious and presumptuous witches that ever were known in this age' were hanged and burnt at the top of the town.

There was a kind of feeding frenzy as folk pressed in to get to the best spot, as the witches were unloaded from the cart and led by burly guards to the 'New Drop', as it was called. Once, the doomed were pushed off a cart to swing until they stopped twitching; now, a new-fangled trapdoor was used – the latest in public execution technology.

The crowd roared like an angry sea as the witches were spotted, stepping up to the platform. Here the hooded hangman waited – a solid, dark figure – next to the priest, also in black, his white collar standing out in the greyness. With some disdain he appealed to the women to repent, to call upon God for mercy. In reply to his supplications, the minister received damning and cursing. Shaw and Philips turned the air blue in such an alarming way that the minister blanched and the crowd gasped.

Scowling, the minister nodded to the hangman, who hooked the nooses over their heads. As the rope was placed over Elinor's neck – still slender and fair – she asked to make confession.

The minister nodded, the hangman loosened the rough rope, and Elinor began to speak to a crowd that fell silent. Only an unkindness of ravens could be heard in the air of that dark and mild day.

'We lived together in one house. We contracted with the Devil about a year ago – to sell our souls to him – to enable us to do the mischief we desired against whom we pleased – either in body, goods, or children. That very night three imps came to us as we were going to bed – and, at the same time, the Devil himself appeared to us – '

The crowd gasped in horror. The observant might have noticed a wry smile on the confessor's face as she continued, warming to her theme. 'Yes, Lord Satan himself, in the shape of a tall, dark figure. He told us that these imps would always be at our service – either to kill man, woman, child, hog, cow, sheep, or any other creature – provided we let them suck our flesh every night.' Elinor's voice thickened, darkened. '"If you will pawn your souls to me for only a Year and two months, I will for all that time assist you in whatever you desire." Agreeing to this pact, the Devil bedded us both, and had carnal knowledge of us – not unlike a man, except his embraces were cold, not warm.' There were howls of outrage and indignation. 'The next morning, we sent four imps to kill two horses of John Webb of Glapthorn because he had accused us of being witches.' The witch's statement grew breathless, as she related each sensational detail with increasing pace, like a child boasting to her friends. 'The very same day, the horse were found dead in a pond. The next day, we killed four hogs belonging to Matthew Gorham because he had said we look like witches. Not thinking this revenge sufficient, we sent two imps to kill his girl, four years of age – ' cries of horror rose above the crowd ' – despite the best skill of the doctors to preserve her life. These imps, while destroying other life, kept us in the pink of health. These same imps said to us – in low voices in the night – that we would never fear any ill, or the fires of hell.'

The witch cackled wildly at all this, gazing upon the slack-jawed credulity of the crowd. The more she related, the more saucer-eyed they became.

Yes, she had bewitched Mrs Wise to death, sending her imps, who sucked at the lower parts of her body. Yes, she had enchanted twelve-year-old Charles Ireland, who had been made to bark like a dog. Yes, when she had been taken into custody she had made the jailor dance naked in the prison for a full hour.

Then Elinor paused, and her tone changed. Now that she had their attention she held their gaze and spoke with conviction: the trial had been a mockery, she revealed: her confession – signed when they had been threatened with death and promised release if they signed it. Torture was used – look, here are the marks! – yet the crowd did not seem to be interested. 'Burn them! Hang them!' they called.

The minister implored them to say their prayers. But Shaw and Philips laughed long and loud, calling for the Devil to come to them. The sheriff insisted they should be dispatched as quickly as possible: 'So that being Hang'd till they were almost Dead, the fire was put to the Straw, Faggots and other Combustable matter, till they were Burnt to Ashes. Thus Liv'd and thus Dyed … The Last Witches.'

The tragic tale of persecution (Shaw and Philips were among hundreds of women in Britain wrongly accused of witchcraft and burnt, hanged or drowned) was echoed around the country at one time – especially in East Anglia, the stomping ground of the notorious Matthew Hopkins, the so-called Witchfinder General.

SIX

THE GHOSTLY LOVER
OF BOUGHTON GREEN

Boughton Green has long been thought an eerie place – one look at the ruined church of St John the Baptist, a gothic pile enshrouded in ivy, deep within an overgrown graveyard, confirms it. The Green, once the site of a notorious horse fair, is said to be haunted by highwaymen and brigands – Cap'n Slash and other such ne'er-do-wells who have mayhap left a psychic stain on the place. The large earth labyrinth of the Shepherd's Race may have long gone – ploughed over during the Second World War – but the lonely triangle exudes a sense of mystery still. Anyone walking along the gloomy back lanes, perhaps making their way home late at night to the nearby village of Moulton, would rightly feel a bit jumpy, as the thoroughfare passed the flanks of the crumbling boneyard. And they would be wise to, for it is haunted by a beautiful but deadly ghost.

According to the received wisdom, the most hazardous time to pass by is Christmas Eve.

There was once a young man foolish enough to do so (isn't there always?).

It was 1875 and William Parker, a young and single farmer, staggered home after a merry evening with friends at a pub in Moulton. His friends had ribbed him as he had left the inn at Moulton, but he had brushed them off, in a show of drunken bravado. 'Old wives' tales!' he had laughed. With a wave and a hiccup he had bid farewell to his drinking buddies – also in their cups, and in full voice. The slurred carols and the ruddy glow from the mullioned windows soon faded as he made his way along the dark lane.

Above, the stars glittered in the vast winter's night. Parker's breath froze before him. Now and then he would chuckle to himself at some humorous incident from the evening. The prospect of a soft bed and perhaps a little night-cap lured him on.

Turning the corner, he was relieved to see the Green before him – just beyond it, and he'd reach the edge of town. St Johns loomed over him, a dark silhouette against the stars. Following the stone wall around, he passed the entrance to the churchyard – the old gate creaking and banging by itself. He laughed at this. Another night, it might have rattled him – but nothing was going to ruin his merry mood this evening.

Tipping his hat, he wished the residents of the churchyard 'Happy Christmas!'

Just then, from out of the shadows, Parker was tickled to be approached by an attractive red-headed lady – her long hair flowing over her pale neck and shoulders like a river of blood. He was instantly beguiled by her, not thinking it strange that she should be loitering in such a lonely and dangerous place by herself.

'Why, hello. A lovely evening for a stroll, is it not, Miss … ?'

The pale lady did not reply, but she smiled and stared at Parker in a way which made his blood warm – as though he had taken a swig of brandy.

In the distance he heard the bell at Moulton chime in Christmas. 'Midnight! Merry Christmas!'

He just so happened to have a sprig of mistletoe on him and he was eager to use it – the beautiful woman needed little prompting.

They kissed – her lips were cold, but the effect was intoxicating. Was that blue light crackling from them? And what was that uncanny fire in her eyes? Parker was spellbound.

They arranged to meet the following month. He promised he would be there – come hell or high water.

The young lady smiled.

As the beauty departed – back into the churchyard – she made no sound, even as she passed through the rusty kissing gate. Parker might have thought this odd any other time, but he was tipsy and smitten. He couldn't believe his luck!

Continuing along the dark lane, he whistled as he went home.

In the morning he awoke groggily. The memory of the kiss warmed him at first, but then, as he sobered up, he realised the whole encounter smacked of the uncanny. Growing pale, he remembered the local warnings about passing by Boughton Green on Christmas Eve.

He told all he met of his chilling encounter with the red-haired woman. Some shook their heads and laughed at him, but the old 'uns nodded slowly and looked at Parker with a knowing sadness.

Within a month he was dead, causes unknown.

Perhaps he had made the tryst after all.

It seems Parker had fallen prey to the charms of an eighteenth-century girl who had committed suicide in the churchyard, after the sudden death of her husband, shortly after their wedding day … at the church. It was said anyone walking by would meet her, or her husband, depending on their gender and fall under their fatal spell.

As a footnote to the site, Boughton Spring has long been renowned for its pure quality and unfailing flow: 'It never runs but in mighty gluts of wet, and whenever it does is thought ominous by the county people, who, from the breaking out of that spring, are wont to prognosticate dearth, the death of some great personae, or very troublesome times.' (Morton, Natural History of Northampton, *quoted by Sternberg in* The Dialect and Folklore of Northamptonshire.*)*

SEVEN

THE
MISTLETOE BRIDE

It was Christmas Eve at Titchmarsh Castle – the traditional time for games of hide and seek in the Lovell household. The halls were decked with boughs of holly and mistletoe, the goose was basting in the oven, the tree was decorated and dominated the main entrance hall, logs crackled in the hearth, and trays of sherry and mince pies were passed around by the servants – neat in their black and white uniforms, 'like polished chess pieces' one waggish uncle joked, red face and overly whiskered.

It was a time of especial festivity, for the young lord and lady of the manor had just been wed, only a couple of days before on the winter solstice.

With a pagan thrill, they had kissed under the mistletoe, and she had held some of the golden bough in her bouquet, and so became known as the Mistletoe Bride.

The bride had looked like the Queen of Winter herself, all in white against the white snow.

Fleet-footed and filled with excitement, the bride was the first to hide. Heart beating wildly, she ran to the top of the house and she finds an old oak chest in the attic. 'Perfect!' she thinks.

She hears the muffled voice of the seeker down below. 'Ready or not, here I come!'

'They'll never find me up here,' she thinks with the frisson of schoolgirlish naughtiness.

She climbs in, and as she does so the lid snaps shut behind her with sickening finality.

At first she is just glad to be hidden away so well, but the thought of the catch niggles at her.

A tiny bit of light seeps through the crack and she gropes along looking for the latch, only to discover, to her horror, that it can only be opened on the outside!

She struggles and starts to scream, hoping someone will come to find her, thoughts of hiding long gone. But there is not much air, and she starts to grow hot and faint. Suddenly, she swoons and it all grows dark, so terribly dark – the darkness of a midwinter night.

The unfortunate newlywed is not found until several years later. By this time, the Lovell legend is enshrined – of the Mistletoe Bride.

In 1242, Sir John Lovell of Minster Lovell married Maud de Sidenham, whose family home was Titchmarsh Castle. Shortly after the marriage, they came to live at the castle, which replaced Minster Lovell in Oxfordshire as their main family residence. Their son, and heir, was born there in 1255, and the family line continued for several years. By 1363, however, the castle had long been deserted and described as 'ruinous'; the rubble was used to build local houses, and only the earthworks are visible today. The Lovell family lost its land at Titchmarsh because of their association with Richard II, who was deposed by Henry of Bolingbroke (anyone associated with him would have fallen out of favour with the new regime, and would lose Crown lands once gifted to them).

Although the wedding reception happened in Oxfordshire and the bride clearly did not die that night, we must allow for artistic license in such matters. Kettering artist and poet, George Harrison, transferred the scene of the wedding celebrations to Titchmarsh. Prior to this, Thomas Haynes Bayley (1797–1839) had immortalised the tale in the popular Victorian ballad 'The Mistletoe Bough'. I have re-imagined the tale in its Victorian setting.

EIGHT

THE WOODMAN AND THE THREE WISHES

Old Tom had been a woodsman of Salcey for as long as any in the area could remember. He knew those woods like the back of his hands – which happened to be as gnarled and weathered as an old tree from the hard work he'd done with them.

One day, he went into Salcey to fell a tree – an old oak which had been marked for felling, for its timber was worth a great deal. It saddened him to topple such a mighty king of the woods, but there you go. He had to make a living. But as he lifted up his axe to strike the trunk, a little voice called out, 'Stop, stop, all your chop, chop!'

The woodsman looked down and there was a fairy jumped out – knee-high, fists on hips, yellow waistcoat, blue britches and red in the face. 'This is my home! Please don't fell it, you look like a kind fellow.'

Well, Old Tom knew better than to get on the wrong side of the Good Folk. He doffed his cap, and begged the little man's pardon; 'Old Tom will fell no fairy oak.'

'Master Tom, you're a good old sausage. You may have wishes three – make them any time you need them.'

'Thank you, your lordship!'

The fairy vanished and Old Tom took his axe on his shoulder and wandered back, tingling all over with the thrill of the encounter.

Dusk fell, and on his way home to his wife, Old Tom plain forget about the fairy and the wishes.

He said hello to his wife as he entered their simple but homely home.

'You're in a good mood.'

Old Tom couldn't say why, but a warm glow filled his heart.

Later, he sat by the fire with a satisfied sigh, the cat purring on his lap, the clack of his wife's knitting needles, and the crackle of the fire sending him into a nice nap.

Suddenly his stomach growled and he licked his lips, feeling peckish all of a sudden. He muttered that he wouldn't half mind some hog pudding.

No sooner had he said so than there was a sound up the chimney, and down fell a string of sausages at his feet.

'What the blazes! Husband! There's bangers in the fireplace!'

The woodsman picked them up and held one to his nose, savouring it like a fine cigar. 'Well, blow me! I plain forgot. Now, it's all come back. You never guess what happened to me earlier, wife … '

Old Tom related the tale.

Wife gave him one of her looks.

'Old Thomas! You're a forgetful old fool! And a dunce – wasting a wish like that!' Annoyed, she muttered 'I wish 'em were on your bloomin' nose!'

There was a flash, and the bangers went wallop – suddenly they were attached to the woodman's nose.

Old Tom yanked and yanked. 'Ged dem off my dose!'

His wife was apologetic – well, she said, 'Now look what you've made me do!' – but despite her efforts, she couldn't pull them free.

'I wish dese sausages were gone!' he moaned.

The string of bangers vanished in a flash.

Old Tom checked his nose, and all was as it should be.

And that was the three wishes used up!

NINE

FAIRY JIP AND WITCH ONE-EYE

A long time before sensible people like you and I were around, there was a rather nasty witch with one good eye. Now, how she ended up nasty – whether it came about from having one eye, or the other way around – who knows?

Anyway, Witch One-eye, for that is, predictably, what she was known as, developed an all-consuming desire to cook and eat an elf. Maybe she had been hearing all that talk around 'elf foods', who knows, but by-the-by, she had to eat elf.

The first problem, which they didn't teach you in the cookbooks, was how to catch an elf. However, it just so happened that at the top of the hill there lived fairies – in nice little houses, probably one of those co-housing projects, you know the sort. Eco-this and eco-that. Anyway, when she had caught her breath back, Witch One-eye rapped on the door (sustainably sourced timber, of course) of one Fairy Jip. Now, young Jip was young by elf standards (that is, only a few hundred years old – a mere whippersnapper). He had a particular penchant for cherries. Oh, my, how he loved them! Wild cherry, bird cherry, merino cherry, glazed; in pies, flans, cheesecakes, jams, cocktails and Bakewell tarts – he could never get enough of them.

Witch One-eye knocked on his door and called out in her sweetest voice, 'Pretty little Jip, come and see the sack of cherries I, your kind neighbour, have brought you – so large, so red, so sweet, so organic.'

Fairy Jip, well he loved cherries as you know, so he darted out, quick as can be – 'Cherries? Where? Where?'

But wily Witch One-eye was waiting with a sack – an empty elf-sized one – and quickly caught him in it.

Cackling and taunting the poor little thing, she made her way back down the hill. 'Look what I've got! Look what I've got! Look what I've got for my pot!'

On her way back to her witchy hovel, she realised she had to get some other ingredients for her elf-food-feast, and so she unwisely left the sack in charge of a handy woodsman. Off she went, singing tunelessly to herself.

Meanwhile, Fairy Jip persuaded the woodsman to let him go – 'Release me and you'll get some good chopping – the wood will cleave to your axe like a knife to butter.' And so he did. Together they filled the sack with thistles, so the witch wouldn't notice.

Fairy Jip flitted away free, but cherry-less.

The witch returned, thanking the woodsman, and went off to prepare her feast, swinging the sack over her shoulder. On her way home she felt sharp stabbing pains. 'Ay, ay! My lad, you'll pay, when I get you home, for stinging me with your pins and needles!'

Once back, she got a big stick and beat the bag until she thought she had smashed all of poor little Jip's bones to smithereens. 'There, that'll learn you!' But when she opened the sack instead of finding pulped elf, she only found bits of thistle. She howled her rage – smoke pouring out of her ears.

In a fury, she dashed as fast as her bony legs would carry her back up co-housing hill and managed to catch Fairy Jip again using exactly the same trick (he wasn't the brightest elf on the knoll). But on the way down, the same thing happened. Witch One-eye (who was also a bit dim) got distracted and left the elf-sack in charge of a stonecutter. While she was gone the fairy managed to persuade the man to let him go and replace him with broken stones. Off he flitted, like a cherry stone spitted. Witch One-eye carried the sack back and got black and blue for her pains. 'Why, you little rogue! I'll soften your bones good and proper when I get my hands on you!'

A third time she traipsed up the hill (this elf-food thing certainly keeps you fit). Knowing her trick wouldn't work a third time, she assumed the disguise of a pedlar, with a churn on her back. She 'bumped' into Jip in the woods and assuming concern, said, 'Master Redcap, watch out, watch out! Old Reynard the fox is after you! You can hide in my churn for safety if you like.'

'Why, thank you kindly, wandering milk pedlar. I'll avail myself of your shiny churn if you don't mind.' And in he went. Witch One-eye sealed it up good and quick, and, singing to herself, went straight back home.

Once in her hovel, she gave strict instructions to her daughter – for once her wartship had known love – to open the churn and chop off the elf's head. She then rushed into the kitchen and started clattering pots and pans. Now, the witch's daughter wasn't the brightest pin in the pin cushion either. She opened the churn and ordered, in a stern, no-nonsense voice, for Jip to place his head on the chopping block.

Jip pleaded stupidity – which was easy for him – and asked her to show him exactly which position she meant. So, the silly girl did just that and off came her maiden head.

Hiding the body and head in the churn, Fairy Jip quickly grabbed a large pebble and dashed up the chimney as Witch One-eye came back in the room.

Pre-occupied with her cooking, she went over to the big pot on the fireplace – opened the lid to stir the contents, savouring the smell by sticking her nose right over it – and her head right under the chimney. Fairy Jip dropped the large pebble on her head, and – bash and splash – Witch One-eye lost her other eye.

And that taught her a lesson! She never touched elf food again, that's for sure.

Fairy Jip flitted back to his house on the hill.

He never did get his cherries!

This version was included in Notes and Queries *by Thomas Sternberg in June 1852 and was collected in the area by him. The story feels like something from Brothers Grimm, as Sternberg himself notes: '(They are) … so extremely like the German ones, that, with very slight alterations, they would serve as translations.' Whether they originated from the same source – deep in the Wald, and migrated across Europe – or arose independently, who can say? Such stories have been common currency, passed from mouth to ear, for centuries.*

Ten

Meal for the Little Redman

Once, two brothers were reduced by the 'badness of the times' to seek shelter in a hut built in the middle of the forest. There, they survived by poaching the King's Deer, and tasty it was too!

But, the two brothers were not alone in their adversity. The same hard times affected the Fairy Folk of the vicinity.

One day, while one brother went off hunting and the other remained behind to guard their hovel and cook what remained of their meat, in popped a Little Redman who looked rather sorry for himself. Scrawny, you might say.

'Plaze gie me a few broth,' he whined in his tiny voice.

Up the ladder dashed the hunter, to get his hatchet – intent on causing his pitiful guest harm, such was the badness of the times.

But in the meantime, the Little Redman seized the pot from the fire, and makes off with it, laughing like, well, a naughty Little Redman.

The brother gave chase, but the Little Redman led him a merry dance – even while carrying the pot, he was incredibly nimble, and lost his pursuer amid the maze of the tangled wood.

The next day, the same thing happened to the other brother ... the same, but different.

Now, it was the turn of the youngest to stay behind to cook the meal. Knowing what had befallen his eldest brother; he was prepared, though, and hid in waiting – for it is a well-known folk fact that a caught Redman will be forced to take you to his treasure.

The pot was a-bubbling good and proper, its lovely smells curling out the hut into the green wood.

The door creaked and the Little Redman sheepishly entered. 'Plaze gie me a few broth.'

But no sooner had he said these words than the youngest brother grabbed the little fellow, good and hard.

How the Redman wriggled so and pleaded most pitifully, in his tiny voice, but the youngest held tight.

Reluctantly, with much a-huffing and dawdling, the Little Redman took the youngest to an old, old well in an ancient part of the forest, thick with creepers, moss and tangled trunks.

His captive lifted up a rock. 'There ye go, and be happy wi' it!' said the Little Redman with a sigh, revealing a glittering crock of gold. Gold like the sun! Gold enough for both the brothers, and to make the youngest a man for life.

The Little Redman seems to be cousin of the Scottish Redcap and the Irish Fir Darrig, all of whom seem to have hidden treasure, suggesting they are guardians of place. Gnomes are thought to be the elementals of the earth and all of its glittering riches, of which Gaia gives so freely. Perhaps from this tale we glean compassion for those in need. Also, to honour the ancient laws of hospitality.

ELEVEN

THE FARMER
AND THE BOGLE

A farmer once encountered problems when he went to mow his new field: a bogle popped up, all twisty horns and brimstone, and said, 'Baint yours, 'tis mine!'

Well, the farmer had bought it fair and square, so he wasn't going to let go of it that easy, was he? He was a wily 'un, and said, 'Let's make a deal – you have one half of the crop, and I'll have the other. Which 'un you'll have?'

The bogle frowned and scratched his warty head. 'Um, the top half.'

The farmer outwitted him and planted potatoes, so when it came to harvest time, the bogle was left with just the stalks.

'Next year I want the bottom halves!' the bogle said.

Well, that canny farmer, what did he do? He planted wheat and the bogle was left with the stubble and he was none too pleased, I can tell you.

So they met up once more and the farmer, seeing the bogle was most niggled, offered him this deal: 'Tell you what, to be fair, next year, let's have a mowing match. Side-by-side, half the field each, and whoever finishes their half quicker can have the lot, for keeps.'

The bogle agreed, and, muttering, vanished.

The wily farmer planted wheat and in secret laced half the ground with iron spikes. You have to get up early to catch him out!

It came to the morning of the mowing match. 'Which side do you want? This side or this?' asked the farmer.

The bogle looked hard.

'You'll try to trick me but I won't let you catch me out. I'll have the one you don't want me to have!' And he pointed to the first.

'You're a sharp 'un, but fair's fair. Pick your tool and let's mow. No stopping till midday. Agreed?'

The bogle nodded and off they set. It was hard work, sweeping the scythe from side-to-side. With his strong arms, the farmer felled his wheat in great hissing arcs. The bogle struggled to wield the ungainly tool that was twice the size of him. With every sweep, his blade clanged against an iron spike – clang! clang! clang!

'Tis mighty thirsty work – when are we going to stop for a wetting?' asked the bogle, mopping his brow.

'No break till midday, as we agreed!'

The bogle threw down his tool in frustration. 'I can't go on! You have the whole rotten lot! I don't want anything to do with your stinky meadow anyhow!' And with that the bogle vanished in a belch of black smoke and that was the last the farmer saw of him.

This is one of the very first stories I learnt, when I was working on a show called 'The Storyteller's Fairy Trial', back in the early 1990s in Northampton. The show didn't happen – but the story did! (I performed it on Frog Island, Becket's Park). Sternberg informs us that the legend is 'Very commonly narrated in Northamptonshire'.

TWELVE

JACK THE WOLF KILLER

A beast lurked in the woods near Badsaddle. For several months now, savaged livestock had been found by distressed farmers and workers. Nearby, the mangled corpses of sheep, cows and goats giant paw-prints had been found – like a hound's, but bigger. Then, one moonlit night, there was the howling. The word was on everyone's lips, but nobody dared speak it.

Wolf! There was a wolf in the woods!

Suddenly, every green shadow seemed sinister. Maids hurried quickly home, clutching their cloaks and baskets tightly to them. Grandmothers were left unvisited. Fires grew thinner as the weather got colder, for no one liked to gather firewood. Children were forced to play close to home. Some were tied to their mother's apron strings for safekeeping. No one hung around to gossip for long at the village pump. Folk grew twitchy and suspicious. Outsiders were discouraged from visiting Badsaddle, with crudely daubed signs which warned them they were entering 'wolf-country'.

Something had to be done – a village meeting was called. Folk gathered in the tithe barn, the air filled with alarm and noisy debate. Everyone had a hairy anecdote. And everyone had an opinion about what should be done, but no one could decide who should do, 'what needed to be done'.

Then, a young man stepped up onto a pile of grain-sacks. He tried to speak above the hubbub, but could not be heard. And so he let out a wolf howl.

Silence.

Wild-eyed panic threatened to take over the crowd, but it was somewhat undermined by laughter.

Everyone stared at the young man, chuckling to himself at the bug-eyed Badsaddlers.

'I'll go and kill it.'

It was young Jack. He had always been the cocky sort, but perhaps now he was showing his true colours. He will save the day!

A few people sneered, snorted with derision, or made snide comments. But the lord of the manor stepped up to Jack, clapped him on the back, and handed him a sword. 'Good lad.' he said, raising his sword-arm. 'Let's hear it for Jack of Badsaddle, our very own wolf killer!' Folk cheered. Jack was buried under an avalanche of hugs, handshakes and kisses. Tankards were thrust into his free hand. Suddenly, he became very popular with the women … He had quite a night that night, let me tell you.

Yet at dawn, in the cold light of day, things seemed different. His mouth was furry, his head throbbed. He guzzled down water like a rabid canine.

'Hair of the dog?' quipped one of the local wags, watching him as off he set, sword over his shoulder, to kill the wolf.

It was a foul day to be setting off into the woods – bitterly cold, biting you could say. Fat snowflakes swirled out of the sky and began to settle on the branches. Jack pulled the heavy cloak around his shoulders, the hood over his head, and ventured into the green shadows, following the old track into the woods.

Jack tracked the wolf for several days, but he quickly discovered that it was hard being a hero. Walking for miles and miles, trudging through deepening snow; freezing nights huddled by lonely fires, flinching at the flickering shadow,;dwindling rations and a growling stomach. But worst, the images of what might happen when he finally met his foe tormenting him. Nightmares of fangs and talons haunted him; being disembowelled by a slathering wolf leaping from the undergrowth; being dragged back to its lair, half-alive, to be eaten bit by bit.

The snow didn't help his tracking at first – but new paw prints emerged on the virgin covering, leading him deeper and deeper into the woods. Sometimes, a bloody trail made it even easier to follow – the latest victim of those murderous jaws.

Finally, Jack came to dark cave. All the tracks led there. From inside issued a foul smell – rank and musky. The wolf's lair.

Jack unsheathed his sword – the steel, cold in his hands. Whether he was shaking from the chill air or from fear, it was hard to tell. There was no one there to see.

No one else would do this deed.

It was down to him and him alone.

Crossing himself, Jack ventured into the dripping darkness … His foot struck something. A bone. A human skeleton.

Jack's heart pounded, and his courage left him – he would have bolted there and then, but it was too late.

First, he heard the growl – thunder in the dark, turning his innards to water. Then, in the bowels of the cave, yellow eyes stared out.

A monstrous wolf – as tall as him to the shoulder – slinked out of the darkness, slowly circling his prey with a low growl, fangs bared. Then, it leapt. There was a blur of fur, fang, and steel.

Jack thought of his mother, his father, his baby brothers and sisters. This was for them. If he did not kill this beast, they would live in terror. They would never be safe.

'For Badsaddle!' Jack thrust the old sword into the soft belly of the beast. It let out a howl of pain and fell on top of him, knocking him out as he fell backwards onto the hard stone floor.

Jack awoke, struggling to breathe. The snout of the wolf was pushing into his face – fixed in a frozen death-snarl. He pushed it off with a grunt and stood up, brushing the slobber and grit from him. He was still alive. He had survived!

He looked down at the still steaming body of the wolf. It was old. It's ribs were showing. The green fire died in its eyes, and for a moment Jack felt a strange pang of sadness.

A wind whistled through the cave, making him shudder.

Then all was silent.

Reeling with the victory, he cut off the beast's head and, with some effort, dragged it back with him towards the village. He couldn't wait to share his adventures with his friends and family. He would dine out on this tale for years to come. He would be the toast of the village – Jack of Badsaddle, the wolf killer.

When he finally arrived on the edge of the village, he was exhausted from the effort – and dying of thirst. He went to the village spring. Breaking the ice on the frozen surface, he dowsed his head in chilly waters, rinsing the muck of battle from him – the blood and mud. Then he took a deep draught of the spring water.

He stood up, smacking his lips, and wiping them with the back of his sleeve. Then, as he turned to go, a pain shot through his body. The water, the water was so cold.

Jack fell to his knees, confused. 'What …?'

He looked down at his belly – a damp stain was spreading over his tunic. It was shredded by claw marks. He pulled it aside – and saw the water leaking, leaking from his belly.

Gasping in agony, he keeled over, writhed and kicked for a moment – then lay still.

The snow fell on the form of Jack of Badsaddle, his sword by his side, the wolf's head looking at him.

And that is how they found him – Jack of Badsaddle, the killer of the last wolf in England. He was buried in the church at Orlingbury, with a fine stone effigy, as grey as a wolf, bearing his name – and his legend lived on, long after the memory of wolves haunting the wild woods had faded and it was safe to walk in the green shadows – safer, but sadder. The wild became tamed, and something in us died – but there are still some in this land who have a wolf in the thickets of their heart.

The man who killed the last English wolf is said to be buried beneath his effigy in Orlingbury Church, dated 1375. There is an alternative version of the story in which a young forester saves the King's life from a wild boar and is granted the freedom of the forest. This was said to have taken place in 1328 and the man was John de Withmayle, known to his friends as Jack. He was knighted Sir John of Orlingbury and was laid to rest, after a long and worthy life, in the church where his tomb remains. I know which version I prefer! How about you?

THIRTEEN

THE DUN COW
OF STANION

In Stanion Church there is an unusual relic – an enormous bone, six-foot long, that looks as though it once belonged to a mythical beast, and, in a way, it did. Once, according to local legend, it belonged to the Dun Cow … The legendary Dun Cow! Have you not heard of it? No? Well, you will now!

One day, the Dun Cow appeared in the village – just strolled right in, bold as brass, or as lackadaisical as a daisy. Folk were even more astonished when it began to speak. It introduced itself politely (don't you know all cows are polite?) and promised milk to all in return for kindly care.

It was too good to be true – where was the catch? Thatcher the grocer said. But the Dun Cow was as good as its word, and milk flowed freely from its udders for all who came to the village green, where it was happily ensconced, munching on buttercups.

This white fountain of goodness became the heart of the community, as folk queued up with their pales, chatting and laughing as they waited in line. Drovers and horsemen passing by, wondering what all the fuss was about, would be offered a ladle of creamy milk and realise why. Many a fine gentlemen lifted his hat to those udders.

And so, the cow's fame spread far and wide.

Until one day a local witch got wind of this miraculous cow. Was she envious of its attention? Did she feel that she was underappreciated? Perhaps she had a chip on her shoulder, or was just stuck in her story – who knows? But the fact is, one morning the witch appeared, produced a sieve from under her cloak, and, much to everyone's astonishment – for the usual queue had formed, which the witch had promptly walked straight by – and ordered the cow to fill it. The villagers cried out in consternation but the kind-hearted bovine could not deny any request. The poor animal strained to keep its promise – literally. No matter how much it expressed itself, it could never fill the sieve for long. All of its efforts drained away, again and again. In the end, dreadfully depleted of its white magic, that noble beast died of exhaustion.

The witch picked up her sieve and, cackling to herself, she sauntered off, followed by everyone's withering stares. Villagers fell by the cooling body of their benefactor, sobbing at its demise.

However, the practical amongst them organised a feast, and even those who shed a tear enjoyed the finest steaks ever. The remains were buried at Cow Common. One rib was preserved as a memorial, which remains to this day in the local church – firm evidence of the remarkable Dun Cow of Stanion.

This legend was recorded in a poem by David Townsend, the village blacksmith at Geddington, three miles from Stanion, around the turn of the old century. The bone is in all likelihood that of a whale, brought back by an adventurous mariner to his native village at the beginning of the seventeenth century, when the edges of the world were still being filled in and it was not inconceivable to think 'here be dragons', or, in Stanion's case, a mythical cow. The villagers have milked this myth for all its worth ever since. The church is kept locked, and you need to ring the local sexton to arrange access to this legendary relic (a similar bone and tale is to be found in St Mary's, Redcliffe, Bristol).

FOURTEEN

THE TREASURE
OF SILVERSTONE

Silverstone racetrack is famous across the world for the motor-racing events held there. The roar of Formula One cars and the excited commentary on the tannoy now carries across the meadows – where once the deep throb of fighter and bomber planes could be heard, for it used to be a Second World War airfield. From its level fields, brave young pilots would take their chances in the skies above Europe. The airfield had been constructed on a site of the former Luffield Abbey – traces of which were visible until then, and for centuries local folk lived and worked amid its ruins.

One such fellow was a farmer named Saywell, who worked the land and led a quiet life. Then, in 1740, Saywell was plagued by deer from Whittlewood – the tract of woodland on his doorstep. A rum place, it was thought. Many a strange doing took place there, by all accounts, and Saywell preferred the common sense and safety of his sensibly flat fields. But those deer were laying waste to his crops, and so he set about catching the culprits. He lay in hiding one night, waiting for them to show their faces – and that's exactly what one of them did.

The herd of wayward deer appeared, sweeping across his fields, stopping to nibble this or that now and again, always on the lookout. One in particular was strange in appearance, having the 'face of a man'.

Curious. His features riveted Saywell so. The deer-man seemed to speak to him, but what he was saying, Saywell could not tell. So, he climbed down from his hide and slowly approached – but as soon as he came near the whole herd vanished – not simply leaping away, but blinking out like a snuffed out wick.

Disturbed and intrigued, Saywell returned the following night and the same thing happened. A third night Saywell found himself there – he couldn't get the face of that man out of his mind. But the deer always disappeared, exactly on the same spot.

Saywell stood there, scratching his head. There was a meaning to this mystery, if only he could fathom it. He looked at the ground beneath his boots.

Finally, the penny dropped.

Taking the hint, Saywell dug there and found a chest. Excitedly, he opened it and was dazzled by the treasure contained within – such shiny pretty things. Saywell realised it must have been hidden by the monks of Luffield in times of trouble. There was one item in particular which stood out – it gleamed in the moonlight in an uncanny way – and as he held it up, Saywell thought he saw the features of the deer-man reflected in it, but perhaps it had just been a trick of the light.

What this treasure consisted of, Saywell kept to himself. But perhaps there is a clue in the title of the place … Silver-stone.

The etymology of Silverstone is intriguing, possibly offering a clue to this mystery. Silverstone seems to have derived from the name, Sigewulf's tūn. A village close by is called Syresham, which may have originated from Sigehere's hām (recorded as Sigresham in the Domesday Book). Sigehere and Sigewulf could have been related. Eleanor J. Forward submitted to the University of Nottingham her thesis, titled 'Place-names of the Whittlewood area', in which she identifies the etymology and adds:

> *It is of added interest that the [villages of Silverstone and Syresham] are geographically close to one another, separated only by the parish of Luffield (Abbey): this could be an indicator that the land around Luffield was originally owned by one man or group and that a proportion of this land was inherited by a descendant, i.e Sigewulf and Sigehere may have been connected to one another (perhaps as father and son). Repetition with variation in Anglo-Saxon times worked in the same way as our modern equivalent, surnames; for example, five of Æthelwulf's children repeated his prototheme (e.g. Æthelstan, Æthelbald). Kitson suggests that people with dithematic names were higher in the social scale (2002:101).*

Could the treasure Saywell discovered be actually Sigewulf's? And could Saywell himself be a descendant. Is it too great a leap to suggest Saywell is a derivative of Sigewulf? Could the treasure he discovered actually have been his own inheritance? Perhaps in the face of the deer Saywell saw the ghost of his ancestor.

FIFTEEN

THE HAUNTED BATTLEFIELD

Charles I's disastrous defeat at the Battle of Naseby might have been avoided if he had heeded a ghostly warning. A legend tells that while the Royal army stayed in Daventry, the King – sequestered in a local inn, the best accommodation that could be secured for him that evening – was visited by the ghost of an old friend, the Earl of Strafford. The phantom pleaded with him not to engage the Roundhead armies to continue his march northwards. Charles was greatly impressed by the visitation and inclined to heed the ghost's warning, but finally yielded to the advice of his generals.

The battle that followed proved a disaster from which the Royalist cause never recovered.

The room in which Strafford's ghost appeared to the King can still be seen at the Wheatsheaf Hotel in Sheep Street.

The 14 June 1645 was a momentous day in English history. 14,000 Parliamentary troops, led by Fairfax and Cromwell (and wearing boots made in Northampton – although the Roundheads never footed the bill), defeated the 10,000 strong Royalist forces, commanded by Prince Rupert. When the battle finally ended, 4,000 dead lay on the fields of Naseby.

For many years after, on the anniversary, the battle was witnessed being re-enacted in the sky above the site. Other eye-witness accounts describe phantom skirmishes on the killing fields themselves. According to psychogeographer Robert Goodman, a 'feeling of "unease" is experienced by anyone near the field. Some have reported a sensation as if being pushed, but the symptoms ceased as soon as they left the area'. Cromwell's body was said to have been taken back to the scene of his greatest victory in 1658, and the ghost of old Ironshanks was said to roam the fields.

SIXTEEN

I AM NOT
YET READY

The villagers of Passenham, rejoiced when they heard that their cruel landlord, Sir Robert Banastre, was dead. He had an iron heart, they said. He governed his demesne with unbending severity. He expelled long-standing tenants, just to avoid paying Poor Laws dues.

Perhaps he had not always been so harsh, but no one could recall a time when he was otherwise. Surely even he had been an innocent babe once, a bright-eyed boy, a naive youth … but the painful memory of years of cruelty overshadowed anything before. He had been born bad, they said, and that is the way he stayed.

So, when Sir Robert suddenly passed away – keeling over one day, clutching his heart no less – theirs was a collective sigh of relief.

For a while, it was as though spring came early to Passenham.

The villagers' elation was short-lived, however, for within a few hours of his death, something sinister and remarkable occurred.

The village green was abuzz with folk who had gathered to share in the news of Banastre's demise. There was an air of celebration – a jug of cider was passed around and someone struck up a fiddle. There was dancing and laughing – things not seen in Passenham, in public, for many a year. But all that came to a sudden stop when a strange clanking noise was heard, approaching down the High Street.

As one, the villagers turned to see what was causing the extraordinary sound.

An armour-clad figure appeared, stiffly walking the lane with a clank and a clonk. A full-faced visor hid the wearer. Only one person was rich enough to have such a suit of armour – Sir Robert.

Two burly farmers approached the figure – 'Oi! Where are you going so fast, tin-shanks?' They were swept to one side by his mighty metal arms.

The villagers watched aghast as the figure continued walking along. No one wanted to approach it now, but together they followed, at a safe distance. Then it stopped in front of a cottage, kicked opened the gate, broke down the door and clomped noisily up the narrow stairs to stand by the bedside of a former tenant of Sir Robert.

Then the suit of armour continued on and did the same at the next house, and the next. Then it vanished.

Well, that rattled the good folk of Passenham, I can tell you. But things settled down, as they often do, even in the strangest of circumstances, for a few days at least.

Then, on the day of Sir Robert's burial, the sexton – finishing off the plot – was startled into fits when the sinister figure in armour appeared again. He was frozen to the spot, trapped in the grave, as the metal man towered over him and lifted up the lid of his beaver to reveal a grisly visage – the pale features of Sir Robert himself. Looking over his half-dug grave, Sir Robert's ghost said, 'I am not yet ready.'

When the sexton had recovered from his faint he told the parish priest, who decided that the sooner Sir Robert was in the ground, the better.

Half the village gathered in the church on the day of Sir Robert's memorial service – not to pay their respects, as such, but to make sure he was a good six foot under. With some trepidation, the parish priest began the burial service, but halfway through he stopped dead: a loud, persistent banging was coming from inside the coffin. Then, the muffled but familiar tones issued from the willow casket, 'I am not yet ready.'

On inspection, the corpse exhibited the usual symptoms of mortality, but after burial his ghost continued to terrify the district.

His cry now changed to, 'Beware! Be ready!'

A service of exorcism was held by the bishop, with bell, book and candle. Right in the middle, Sir Robert appeared in a flash of light. He begged the bishop to stop. He promised to desist from further hauntings if the service was terminated. The bishop, trembling with fear, agreed, and Sir Robert has kept his promise for three hundred years.

Contrary to his legend, Sir Robert Banastre, buried beneath his monument in St Guthlac's Church, Passenham, is recorded as being a man of singular piety and a great benefactor of the local church. Yet local tradition remembers him as an evil, grasping tyrant who expelled tenants to avoid payment of Poor Laws dues. For this he was supposedly condemned to an uneasy death and a restless, miserable existence in the hereafter.

SEVENTEEN

THE
RESTLESS GHOST

Goodman William Clark, 'Bill the Brewer' to his friends, was a malster. He always smelled of hops, for it was his profession to make them for the malt. He lived in a farmhouse in Hannington – Old Pells' place – four country miles from Northampton town. He was happy enough in his life. He had a wife and little 'uns, who were enough to keep him on his toes!

Things had been (relatively) peaceful in the Clark household until recently, when the Clarks had been often rudely awakened in the night by not only bumps, but other strange doings. The doors, which he habitually bolted before turning in, were found unlocked, unbolted, and sometimes flung off their hinges.

One night, Clark, grumbling as he got out of bed, pulled his nightshirt down his skinny legs, bristling with goosebumps, and took the candle in its holder, a-guttering and a-muttering down to the disturbance. There he found one of the mullioned windows all smashed in, as though the very Devil had been abroad!

The next night it happened again. At the end of his tether, Clark got up like a shot and dashed downstairs with a poker, ready to apprehend the villain once and for all. The front door was flung open. It was still moving – as though someone had just scarpered – and so Clark bolted out into the night in hot pursuit. 'Where the blazes are you? Come out, you devil!'

A short distance from the house he was startled by a ghostly visage – the phantom of a man in antique clothing, like a figure from a painting. The light of the moon shone visibly through him, as though he was a bed sheet on the line. At first, Clark was affrighted – his bony knees knocking together – but he called out to the Almighty to protect him. 'What are you? What do you want?'

To his surprise, the apparition smiled and, in a clear, friendly voice, spoke these words: 'I am the disturbed spirit of a person long since dead. I was murdered near this place two hundred and sixty seven years, nine weeks, and two days ago. Come along with me and I will show you where the foul deed was done.'

Clark found his curiosity overcoming his fear, and he followed the phantom into the next field, to the side of a hedge. The ghost stopped over a particular spot and spoke once more: 'Here I was killed! Here, my head was cruelly separated from my body.' He showed Clark by lifting up his head from his shoulders. Point proven, the ghost positioned it back on its stump of neck.

When he recovered a little from the grisly sight, he spluttered a question, 'Who did this? Why?'

The phantom replied, 'The perpetrator is long turned to dust. They did it for greed – a neighbour coveted my estate. He offered me money, he threatened me, and, when I wouldn't give in' – he let out a sigh from his neck – 'he killed me.'

Clark, growing bold and curious, asked where the ghost formerly dwelled, and to his surprise it told him it was in Southwark, London. There, it explained, it had left some money and some writings buried in the earth. It had prayed upon his mind. Until his treasure was dug up and disposed of 'according to his mind' he would never be at rest.

Clark, warming to the theme – which was becoming increasingly interesting – asked why the ghost hadn't stirred from the grave before. Why had he waited so long?

The ghost explained that he had haunted and disturbed the place of his murder for several years after the deed, but a friar (whose name was quickly forgotten) exorcised him – binding him from restlessness for a full two hundred and fifty years.

But, with that time being up, he was free to roam once more. Two and half centuries he had waited! He would not rest until someone did as he desired – dig up the treasure and distribute it according to his wishes.

Clark, keen to have peace restored to his home once more, agreed to undertake this task.

The ghost bid him go to London that very next day, but Clark said this was impossible if he wasn't to lose business and put matters straight first. He had his family to consider. He couldn't just up sticks at the drop of a hat (or head). It would take him a fortnight to arrange such a trip. Very well, the ghost conceded – they shall meet in a fortnight's time in London, on London Bridge. 'Do you give your word, Goodman Clark?'

He did and the ghost vanished.

Clark returned to his bed, unable to sleep. His wife wondered what had disturbed him so and he explained all, to her saucer-eyed astonishment. Then, the next morning, he told his neighbours and the Minister of the Parish and anyone else he passed in the street. All advised him to keep his word – but not to eat or drink anything in that place. So, within a fortnight, he set off for London.

The ghost appeared to him several times during those two weeks, but seemed to be in good spirits – if you can excuse the pun – seeing Clark preparing to make good his promise. The peculiar pair – phantom and man – talked freely now, most evenings, like old friends. Slowly, they became acquainted and Clark discovered that the ghost had left a wife and two children, and the ghost's estate had survived through several generations. When Clark asked questions, however, about the status of the spirit's soul – and whether it dwelled in joy or torment – it kept as silent as the grave.

The day finally came, and on Saturday, 9 January, Goodman Clark set off for London, enduring the roads of winter in a chilly stagecoach. By Sunday afternoon he found himself stepping onto the bridge at Southwark – somewhat fatigued from his journey, but excited about what awaited him. He lingered on the bridge for a while, but the ghost did not show. It seemed so improbable, in the middle of a busy London. Had it all been moon dreams?

Yet, when Clark walked slowly off the bridge towards Southwark, from a shady alley he felt an icy presence, and there was his old friend. Now, the spirit appeared more flesh-like. It led him – in broad daylight – to an obscure lane. For a while they stood outside a house, but the ghost seemed reluctant to go in, explaining that two strangers were present who were not concerned with his business.

He waited for them to go, and then they visited the house in which two women lived. At first, they were suspicious of this strange pair – a country brewer with the smell of hops about him, and a rather pale-faced gentleman with somewhat archaic manners. Yet, the smooth-tongued ghost talked his way and soon they were sitting in the parlour explaining their story. The women grew sceptical until the ghost put his hand through the teapot. Now believing him, they allowed the ghost to lead them to a certain spot in their yard. He bid them dig there the next day. He said that he would return at noon the next to supervise, before he vanished before their eyes.

Goodman Clark arranged for lodging, and returned the next day with a spade. The ghost appeared and bid him dig. He got stuck in

as the two women looked on with great curiosity. Breaking a sweat, he stopped to rest on his spade and mop his brow. 'Go on,' the ghost insisted. 'Deeper!' Grumbling, Goodman Clark continued until he had dug eight feet down – and then, his spade struck something solid and hollow. He asked for a lantern to see in the pit. Clearing away the earth, he discovered a pot, and, scraping away the soil, gold coins gleamed within. Suddenly, his exertions seemed worthwhile. The pot was lifted out and cleaned off. It broke apart. Along with the coins were some papers, but these crumbled on touch.

The ghost was beside itself. No sooner had Clark sat down to catch his breath, the ghost instructed him on how to dispose of the treasure, insisting that he followed his instructions to the letter.

Clark, as good as his word, did so, and the ghost appeared one last time, full of joy, to thank him for his travails. 'Thou has done well, and henceforth, I shall be at rest, so as never more to trouble thee.'

The phantom vanished, and Clark, his strange business finished in London, departed back to Northamptonshire. His family were pleased to see him and to report that no further disturbances had been reported.

This story is all the more remarkable for apparently being true. It was recorded three weeks after the event in a Victorian pamphlet entitled 'The Restless Ghost, or Wonderful News from Northamptonshire and Southwark', claiming to be 'a most true and Perfect Account of a Persons Appearance that was Murdered above two Hundred and Fifty Years ago'. The veracity of this account attests to the validity of the oral tradition if nothing else: 'This Relation is taken from the said Will. Clarks own Mouth, who came to London on purpose, and will be Attested and Justified by Will. Stubbins, John Charlton, and John Stevens, to be spoken with any day, at the Castle Inn without Smith-Field-Barrs, and many others.' So, a good pub story at the very least!

EIGHTEEN

DIONYSIA, THE FEMALE KNIGHT

Skulking Dudley, as he became known – and you'll find out why soon enough – inherited Clopton Manor in the fifteenth century. He was a bit of a clod, by all accounts – of which there were many – and soon he insulted a neighbouring landowner, a young man who challenged him to a duel. The gauntlet was thrown down at his feet. He gulped and turned white – as white as a ghost.

As you might have guessed, Dudley was a coward. He made no bones about it. Some people were born plucky; he was born, well, a plucked chicken.

On the appointed day he took to his bed, feigning illness. To save his honour he sent his own daughter in his place – Dionysia – disguised in armour.

Perhaps making up for her father's ineffectual nature, Dionysia was a no-nonsense sort. She had been a bit of a tomboy growing up, and she had firmed up into a fine figure of a woman, with a sensible head on her shoulders. However, when it came to her father, she had something of a blind spot and so she agreed to his foolish request.

She was strapped into the family suit of armour, which was far too big for her. When the helmet visor was locked into place, she could hardly see through the gap, let alone swing a sword.

'At least no one will know it is you,' explained her father. 'All you need to do is turn up. You won't get hurt in that thing. Just give him a couple of thwacks and have done with it. I'm sure he'll see sense after that.'

And so Dionysia was winched onto her father's horse and, with his tearful blessing, set off to meet her destiny.

Her opponent awaited her on the tilting field, his colourful tent trim – pennant flapping in the morning air. Astride his steed, he held his lance at a jaunty angle. The tendrils of dawn mist curled through the trees like cats. A servant sneezed and blew his nose. Another stomped and rubbed his hands together. The judge of the duel gave them a frosty look and they stood to attention.

Dionysa rode to her end and selected a lance, a nice long pointy one. She struggled to hold it, nearly losing her balance. Her man-at-arms looked at her with a puzzled expression. Someone whispered something about Dudley being drunk again, which made her cheeks burn.

She lined up and waited for the signal, then spurred her steed on. She tried to line up the lance – she had seen it done countless times, commenting on this or that knight, as she had watched with her father and her ladies-in-waiting, stiffling their giggles. If only she had paid more attention to their technique than the cut of their livery, their prowess and reputation!

Her opponent galloped towards her, his lance straightening up and aiming straight at her.

Before she knew it, she had been thrust from her horse by the sudden, painful impact of the lance, which splintered against her breastplate. She fell heavily to the sward, her horse trotting off to nibble peacefully by itself.

The young knight turned his horse around and trotted back. He slowly dismounted, taking his mace and, swinging it viciously, he approached.

'Wait!' she cried, pulling off her helmet. 'Desist, sir, with your metal asterix – you have made your point! I yield.' She brushed the strands of hair from her glaring face.

Her opponent was stunned by this revelation, and he dropped his mace on his foot, which made him yelp. Cursing, he pulled the helmet from his head, revealing darkly handsome features.

Dionysia smiled.

The young man gazed at her, flabbergasted. 'You're … you're … a …'

'A young lady who needs a hand getting up. Would you mind?'

The man stepped forward and pulled her up and she toppled into his arms. Suddenly, their faces were very close together.

'Is there something on my nose?' she asked, for the young man was staring so.

The truth of the matter was Cupid's bow had struck – the erotic dart had twanged home. The young man had fallen instantly in love with her. There was something about a woman in armour that just … did it for him.

He bent his knee (not easy in a suit of armour). 'Will you … marry me?'

'Whoa there, tyger! We haven't even been formally introduced yet. Let me think about it.'

Dionysia did. She considered her options and eventually yielded. They were wed – which resolved the thorny issue of the duel – and they entered into the duel of matrimony.

Her father never lived down his cowardice after that. He became known as Skulking Dudley – but never to his face. Though he often thought he heard folk whispering it as he went passed.

One day, during harvest, he whipped a servant – a particularly cocky one – for being sluggish. He had often been at the receiving end of his lord's brutality, as though he had been selected as the lord's own whipping horse. Since his shameful performance at the duel, Dudley had grown crueller and seemed to take out his inadequacies through a personal vendetta on the man. The man was so enraged by yet another public whipping that he grabbed his scythe and struck off his master's head, which surprised Skulking Dudley a great deal.

Life in the area became peaceful after that for a while. But then, in the dead of night, moaning and rattling was heard, and a headless ghost was seen roaming about, as though it was looking for something. His head, presumably, for indeed it was Skulking Dudley, now living (or rather dying) up to his name more than ever.

The good folk of Clopton had had enough of him in life, and his return was most unwelcome. Matters were taken into hand. It took twelve clergymen to lay the ghost of Skulking Dudley to rest, for he was a most persistent supernatural pest, but finally Clopton returned to its peaceful status quo.

As for Dionysia – those feckless storytellers have forgotten to relate, but I would like to think she lived happily and well, enjoying only the pleasantest bumps in the night. She hung up her father's suit of armour for good, but kept it polished, in memory of when she took to the tourney field and won her man.

NINETEEN

THE FAR-TRAVELLED FIDDLER

In the grounds of Rushton Hall there stands a remarkable structure – Rushton Lodge. It has three floors, three sides, triangular windows, and the whole design is based upon threes, for its owner and designer was Sir Francis Tresham, who was a not-so-secret Catholic and wanted to express his faith in the Holy Trinity with such a building. He was part of the Gunpowder Plot, along with Guido Fawkes and others, and it was thought they had met in the Triangular Lodge to hatch their infamous and doomed plans. Tresham was executed for his part in the attempt to blow up Parliament, but the Lodge survived and eventually passed into the hands of Lord Robert Cullen. Cullen was thrilled to discover a secret underground passage leading from the Lodge. Intrigued as to where it might lead, but nervous about venturing in himself, he offered a reward of £50 to any bold enough to explore right until the end.

The offer was taken up by a local fiddler, who knew a good opportunity when he saw one. Cannily, he accepted the money and gave it to his wife for safekeeping, then into the darkness he ventured, with a candle in his hatband, playing the tune of 'Moll in the Wad', his favourite one. It always brought him luck and as he scraped his bow across his trusty fiddle he hoped it would again.

Cullen and his retinue cheered him on – like Orpheus he was, playing himself into the Underworld (and back, they hoped!). 'Don't eat any pomegranate pips,' Cullen guffawed.

The music faded.

The fiddler ventured a safe distance along the passageway then he blew out the candle. He continued playing for some time, slowly making it fainter and fainter. Then he waited, listening closely. He was a patient man.

He waited, in the dripping darkness. He heard them call him, but he did not reply. There were sounds of someone nervously venturing into the entrance and he froze – but the voice stayed the same distance away, calling him, again and again.

Still and silent, he remained, in the dark, dank tunnel. All he could hear was his heartbeat.

Quietly, the fiddler took a sip from a wineskin offered to him 'for Dutch courage' and waited. He briefly wondered what exactly was down the passageway. He had no intention of finding out.

However, he made himself busy and dug with his knife a pit – deep enough to look unwelcoming – and by it he placed his hat and candle.

He waited a good few hours, getting merry on the contents of the wineskin. When it was late in the evening, he saw the glow of a torch and he heard an owl call – the pre-arranged signal. He replied with a hoot and, smiling, ventured back along the passage. His wife greeted him warmly, offering him some victuals which he heartily received.

They returned in the cover of darkness to their abode. There, the fiddler gathered some belongings and mounted a horse, saddled and ready to go. He bid a fond farewell to his wife and galloped into the night.

On the morrow, the fiddler still hadn't been found. His wife was informed of the sad news, and she ran to Rushton Lodge, wailing in her woe. Cullen soon calmed her with promises of compensation.

And so she lived in comfort – the merry widow.

Two years later, a letter was received. It was from her husband, claiming that he had fallen all the way through the world and had ended up in the newly discovered Australia. The canny fiddler's wife took it to the Lord.

Cullen was so impressed by this – for surely it was evidence of his remarkable passage to the Antipodes, right below Rushton Lodge – that he paid for her passage to Australia to join her husband. She made her plans and sorted out her affairs, and on the appointed day left the village with pomp and ceremony. She was off to join her famous husband, the far-travelled fiddler!

They met at an arranged secret rendezvous – for he had dodged his rescuers and gone into hiding. Finally they were reunited and they danced in joy – as the fiddler struck up his favourite tune, 'Moll in the Wad'.

TWENTY

THE
NAVVY'S TIFFIN

In West Haddon in the nineteenth century there was a wily landlord of a coaching inn who never missed a trick. If he had any opportunity to play a fast one on a passing customer, he always would.

One day, a travelling navvy stopped at the Crown for beer, bread and cheese. Setting his basket down, the landlord notices a freshly caught hare. Licking his lips, he slips away – kills an unfortunate cat (it'd been getting on his nerves for some time) – and when the navvy's attention was elsewhere, substitutes the dead animal for the hare.

After his meal, the navvy sets off on his journey, but after some distance notices the basket is lighter than before.

He opens his basket and – lo and behold! – the navvy discovers that he has been duped. In a fume, he returns to the hostelry on the Sunday morning following, but finds the landlord has gone to church.

Well, he wouldn't be cheated of his revenge.

He asks the serving girl for some small beer, and, as she goes to the cellar, he takes out a leg of mutton from a steaming cooking pot nearby and replaces it with the cat and cheerfully makes his way out – justice done!

He is far away by the time the hungry landlord returns and asks for some mutton broth.

He is surprised that his mutton broth is 'swimming in a great lot of hair'.

He chides the girl, who spills out the story.

Realising what had happened, they give chase – but the navvy is long gone.

This story is based upon a folk ballad written by William Page in 1928. Another sozzled tale, recorded by Richard Braithwait (1588-1673) describes the exploits of an inebriated wayfarer who makes his way from London to Westmorland via Wisbech ('Tales of Drunken Barnaby'). En route, he enters Northamptonshire and drinks his way through the county on the ultimate pub crawl – stopping at Daventry, Weedon, Towcester, and Wansford on the northern border – where he falls asleep on a haystack in a paralytic stupor. Even when it begins to rain heavily, he does not stir. The floodwaters rise and the haystack gets swept into the Nene, with boozy Barnaby on it. Finally, the drunkard awakes and wonders what is happening. He is spotted by some bemused onlookers from the riverbank, who ask where he is from – 'Was he from Greenland?' they asked, perhaps waggishly. 'No!' he responds 'England', thinking he has drifted onto a foreign shore. The event is celebrated at the Haycock Hotel by Wansford Bridge, and recorded in Northamptonshire Notes and Queries *in 1899.*

CAPTAIN SLASH ON CHRISTMAS EVE

It was Christmas Eve in Moulton. A group of somewhat merry gentlemen were discussing serious matters … the apparitions said to appear on the eve of Yuletide at the churchyard by Boughton Green – that notorious haunt of ne'er-do-wells, where the infamous Horse Fair took place over three days every midsummer. The gentlemen listed its many scandalous goings on – the drinking, the fighting, the whoring, the gambling – and the only redemptive feature, that of the running of the Shepherd's Race, the great turf labyrinth in the middle of the green. The stories got saucier and scarier – something about a ghostly lover, and something about the ghost of Captain Slash!

One Boughton Fayre, the infamous brigand, Captain Slash, attempted a robbery, perhaps somewhat drunkenly. He hazarded to rob a shoemaker – not a good idea in a town of cobblers, as they were a powerful guild. The victim survived and identified the thief, who was caught and tried, and swung from a gibbet on the racecourse. His ghost is said to haunt Boughton Green.

Among the company of men was a certain Jonas White, a weaver from Kingsthorpe, who, standing up and clomping down his tankard, boldly asserted 'I am not afeared of any mortal man or ghost!'

This was a red rag to the bull for the men present. Robert Bletsoe offered to wager his three-year-old horse against White's pigs that he dared not to set foot in the churchyard at midnight that night. The bet was accepted – the men spat and shook on it.

Unbeknown to either, though, another man in the group decided to play a prank on them all.

The group girded their loins against the chill of the night and the threat of spectres, summoning bravado from their tankards. Taking lanthorns and thick oak cudgels they set off.

Meanwhile, the 'ungodly of Moulton' searched for someone to dress as a ghost, according to the eavesdropper's plan. In The Blue Bell there was found a highwayman, in his bucket boots in booze, who they lured with more liquor to perform their deed.

Leading him to Boughton – spinning him this way and that, so that he did not know where he was – they stripped him of his clothes, smeared his body with honey, and then rolled him in soot, so he looked like a 'poor heathen'.

The drunken sotte was then hidden in a small wood to the north of the churchyard – Little Warren Spinney – to wait until the hour of midnight.

The bells of Moulton finally rang out, and Jonas, ashen faced, knees a-trembling, gulped as he prepared to fulfil his rash boast. He took a skein of thread with him, to help him find his way back in the dark, and ventured forth into the enclosure of the dead. The men of Moulton stirred their drunken ghost into action, and forced him down the other end of the path.

Bletsoe, meanwhile, entered from the eastern end, attired all in white.

Jonas White, seeing this apparition, fell to his knees in terror, hiding behind a gravestone, face to the earth, praying for salvation.

However, the ghost in white now beheld the figure in black and, thinking it must be the ghost of the notorious Captain Slash, fled, arms waving and uttering fearful cries, towards where the men of Moulton lay in hiding.

They, supposing him to be a ghost, fled for their own lives back home, where, with wide-eyes, they told of the ghostly vision they had seen, narrowly escaping with their lives.

The drunken highwayman— so overcome with liquor he felt no fear – walked up the path to the watchers of Kingsthorpe. They, seeing a figure all in black approach – and thinking it was the very fiend himself – fled also, without casting a glance back.

The highwayman was found the next morning, sleeping off his hangover from hell in a ditch.

Bletsoe made his way home by devious paths.

And White, after waiting until dawn, ventured home, a chastened man.

In 1826, the notorious highwayman George Catherall or 'Captain Slash' was detained at Boughton Fayre, accused of robbing a shoemaker of eleven half-crowns, one crown, a neckerchief, a corkscrew and a waistcoat. He was subsequently tried and hanged in Northampton on 21 July 1826. His ghost is said to roam Boughton Green and Little Warren Spinney by the ruins of old St John's Church. Boughton Green is a roughly triangular piece of land by the ruins of old St John's Church, which was once surrounded by the medieval village of Boughton.

A charter of 1353 granted permission for an annual three-day fair on Boughton Green to celebrate the nativity of St John the Baptist; woodcrafts and agricultural implements were sold on the first day, festivities with wrestling and horse races on the second, and cattle were sold on the third day. There was a turf maze known as 'The Shepherd's Race', still visible in 1946, but sadly it was ploughed over. The medieval village declined in the late fifteenth to early sixteenth centuries, and St John's Church became ruinous, though the tower and spire were still standing in 1773. The story of the drunken ghosts was originally recorded in the Northampton County Magazine, *although it sets the date of the incident too early (1708) to include the then yet-to-be-born Captain Slash.*

ROBYNE HODE
OF ROCKINGHAM

Hounded by the Sheriff's men, Robin Hood was forced to ply his trade – as outlaw, wolf's head, and liberator of his people – further and further afield these days. Life in Sherwood had become unpeaceful as of late, but fortunately fragments of the wildwood still stretched all the way to the south coast. It was said a squirrel could once leap from branch to branch from Nottingham to the White Cliffs. This ancient woodland had a name lost to all but a few: Anderida. Robin Hood had fled Sherwood until things 'cooled off'. He lay low in the farming woods near Brigstock, feasting on the King's game. A verderer spotted him at one point, but was sent flying, with an arrow or two to chivvy him along.

Then, it possessed Robin to visit the local church – it was St Mary's Day, as good as any to bend his knee before the altar. And so off he set, walking as bold as brass across the fields and into the church.

The congregation grew silent as the priest's sermon petered out at the sight before him. They followed his saucer-eyed stare. In the doorway of the church stood the unmistakable figure of a hundred songs and tales – his bow, his hood, and his horn marked him out as no ordinary outlaw.

'It's Robin Hood!' they gasped.

He swaggered up the aisle, with a smile on his lips, as the parishioners stared open-mouthed at him. The women cast him sly

admiring glances; the men snarled; and the worthies bristled in indignation. He knelt down before the altar and joined in the prayer.

He looked vulnerable to attack, but then folk noticed the band of 'merry men' by the entrance, and a rougher bunch they had never seen.

The priest hesitated, but the merry men carried a freshly killed buck into the church and lay it upon the font. He gulped and carried on.

Grumbling, the congregation reluctantly joined in the service – Robin Hood's voice mingling with theirs.

Then, up in the belfry, there was the moan of the wind – or so it seemed to the congregation. Robin tilted up his hooded head, listening with keen ears. He quickly got up, picked up his bow and was away with his men.

As they burst outside, they were confronted by a hail of arrows – the sheriff's men had found them – but their lookout in the belfry had given them just enough warning. The outlaws provided covering fire, as Much the Miller's Son clattered down the tiles and leapt onto the bank, following his companions as they made good their escape into the green shadows.

Unfortunately, one of the enemy arrows penetrated a window, scattering shards of glass, and hit the priest where he stood. An arrow through his heart, he watched aghast as blood dripped from the arrow head. He crumpled onto the floor at the foot of the altar. The screams of the women and the curses of the men carried across the fields.

Robin Hood paused at the edge of the wood, and looked back – a sad look in his eyes. He raised his horn to his lips, in tribute to the fallen, as much as to gather his men, who came bounding over the fields. The sheriff's men tried to cut them off as they made their way through the stooks of wheat, but they fought bravely. Arrows flew like ears of wheat to the scythe, but Robin Hood withstood the onslaught, giving back as good as he got.

The sheriff's men were led by a figure in armour on horseback – Sir Ralph de Hanville. He had a haughty bearing and bellowed out his orders to his men, driving them on. Robin Hood notched an arrow to his bow and took aim. The death of the priest hung heavily upon him.

Hood fired his bow and his aim was true. It struck home, piercing Sir Ralph's armour. Clutching his side, he turned his horse and fell from it. His men carried him back to the church, where he died next to the body of the fallen priest.

Robin Hood and his men melted into the woods and were not seen in the county again, although by the River Nene, at Ferry Meadows, there stands today standing stones called Robin Hood and Little John – now over the county border. Perhaps it was here the green men made their crossing as they travelled northwards. The outlaw's brief visit to the county quickly became the stuff of legend.

Although it might seem unlikely to some that Robin Hood ventured so far south, Northamptonshire has fine swathes of forest – Rockingham, Salcey, Yardley Chase – which inevitably attracted its share of 'outlaws' (one could become one simply by gathering firewood). This tale is based upon a dubious fragment of 'history'. Robin Hood was said to have secretly visited Brigstock during the reign of Henry II (1216–1272). He entered St Andrews Church, but some of the villagers betrayed him and Ralph de Hanville, a royal official of the manor, sent soldiers to lay siege to the church. During the attack, he managed to escape, but the priest, who was standing by the altar, was killed by an arrow. Charles Montagu-Douglas-Scott in his Tales of Old Northamptonshire *presented it in ballad form, based upon 'Robin Hood and the Monk' written around 1450 from a much earlier oral source. This story is based upon Montagu-Douglas-Scott's version. Many counties have acquired their own Hood-lore in a similar way. There seems to have been several historical 'Robin Hoods' which suggest it was either a common name for an outlaw – a bit like 'Jack-the-Lad', or the prevalence of 'John-sons' and 'Jack-sons', begot in the greenwood at Beltane. It could have been a title, bestowed upon the King of the Wildwood and passed on; or there is the possibility that Robin Hood is a 'Green Man' figure – an archetype, a demigod, as well as a folk hero. This all goes into his particular allure. But if that feels far-fetched then consider the evidence: a 'Robyne Hode' was imprisoned at Rockingham Castle in 1354, for 'trespass of vert and venison in the Forest'. I feel, like the late author Robert Holdstock (author of the 'Mythago Wood' cycle of novels) that such potent figures ever lurk in the green shadows in any ancient woodland, at the edge of our consciousness, closer than you think.*

HEREWARD
IN HIDING

Hereward the Wake, legend of the Fens, moved like a shadow through that flat land of mist and water. He and his men had waged a guerrilla war against the Norman overlords – striking hard, striking fast; always on the run, with cold steel at their back. Yet the common folk were on their side, offering a discreet fire, a bowl of broth, a fresh-straw bed, a tumble with a village girl now and then. But such a life had taken its toll. Their enemy was better equipped, better organised and better disciplined. After the fall of Ely in the autumn of 1071, Hereward vanished from the Fens – for a while at least.

In fact, he had slipped into the remoter parts of Northamptonshire forests to summon more men to his aid.

Amongst his band of outlaws were four Northamptonshire men of steel – at one time, some of the most renowned knights in the kingdom: Tostig and Godwin of Rothwell, Godfricus of Corby and Villicus of Drayton. No doubt, they had many good hiding places and local contacts between them.

Together they passed through the forest of Bruneswald (Bromswold), which bridged the county with Huntingdonshire and Bedfordshire – linking with the three county forests of Rockingham, Salcey and Whittlewood – a wildlife corridor for wolf's heads. Traversing this sylvan labyrinth, Hereward and his men got lost. They had been on the run for several days and were exhausted.

The outlaws collapsed in a shady grove, slumped against trees, hoods and cloaks pulled around them against the interminable rain, which had soaked into everything and sapped their spirits.

They thought of lost comrades, lost loves, family and friends left far behind – the comforts of the hearth now but a faint memory.

Hereward, for once, had no encouraging words. He had spear-headed the resistance for too long – a driven visionary, his energy, his conviction had filled all he came into contact with with his fervour, but even a firebrand can splutter out.

Someone tried to light a fire, but everything was damp. Cursing, the warrior cast down his flint and tinder.

Suddenly, Hereward tensed – he sensed a presence in the shadows. His men immediately picked up on this, and seized their weapons, springing stealthily into action. Hereward scrutinised the under-growth with keen eyes. There was a figure, moving amongst the trees. A fleeting glimpse there. And there!

Silently, Hereward signalled to his men to flank the lurker – cut off his escape. He himself ventured closer to the copse of trees, sword raised in readiness.

Suddenly, the figure stepped into view. It was a man in a robe, with a powerful presence and a commanding gaze which made Hereward lower his sword.

Wordlessly, he slowly approached, mesmerised by this figure who stood before him boldly.

Hereward fell to his knees.

The man emanated an authority, a great sanctity.

Hereward's men found him there, confused as to his behaviour.

Snapping out of his trance, he explained, 'It's Saint Peter himself, did you not see?'

The men scoffed, as they scanned the undergrowth.

Suddenly, a wolf appeared making them all flinch. It was a great grey beast, with amber eyes flashing, fangs bared until Hereward made his men lower their weapons.

The wolf turned and trotted off. It paused, turning to see if they followed. Hereward needed no further prompting; he began to follow the wolf. 'Come on!' he said to his men.

The wolf led them through the wildwood.

'Where the hell is it taking us?' breathed one of his men.

'To freedom,' said Hereward, urging them on.

They had learnt to trust their leader's instincts. Shrugging, they continued.

The wolf led them deeper and deeper into the wildwood until they were completely bewildered, but Hereward trusted in the wolf. Dusk fell and it got harder to see where they were going.

'We need to stop!' called out one of his men, after stumbling for the umpteenth time in the gloom.

'No, we mustn't lose track of our guide.'

And so they pushed on, until it was virtually pitch black and the only light came from the wolf's eyes, like torches in the dark.

Then, ahead, a miraculous sight greeted them. 'Look!' whispered Hereward.

Before them, they beheld candles, flaming into life from every branch.

In hushed awe, the men made their way through the trees. The wolf trotting ahead of them, long tongue lolling.

By daylight the candles had faded, and the wolf was nowhere to be seen. Yet, the men walked out of the wild wood into a clearing on the edge of a village. Blinking in the light of the new day and, looking grizzled, they grinned wolfishly at each other. They were hungry and tired, but alive. None could explain what they had experienced and none of them mentioned it, as if by doing so it would break the spell.

And so they carried on their way, seeking refuge for somewhere to break their fast. Hereward led the way into the village, where a cold ring of Ironheads, William I's soldiers, waited. Before Hereward could flee he was captured. As he was overcome, he blew his horn to warn his men. It was knocked from his lips and he was smashed to the ground. Bloody and dazed, he was roughly led away.

Helpless, his men watched from the green shadows – to attempt his rescue at this point would have been suicide.

Hereward was placed in Bedford Gaol. Things looked grim for the rebel leader: he would surely be executed as an example to all would-be insurgents.

A week later, the outlaw prisoner was escorted to Rockingham Castle with a heavily armed guard. Hereward's men lay in wait in the forest – they had been able to summon more help and plan an attack. They ambushed the guard in a hail of well-aimed arrows, which felled half of the Normans; the rest were finished off in a brief, bloody skirmish.

Hereward was released, and together they melted into the forest, leaving a silent grove filled with still bodies.

A wolf watched on – amber eyes in the shadows. It let out a howl which carried across the unbroken canopy. In the distance Hereward paused and listened. He knelt and thanked the Lord, before carrying on his way.

This was recorded in the Gesta Herewardi (Deeds of Hereward) *a twelfth-century book by an Ely monk known simply as Richard. The tale has a 'Robin Hood' feel to it, and the motif of the King or Hero in hiding, waiting to return to redeem his people, has an archetypal feel. In a way, it could be said that our dormant potential lies in the 'shadows' of our own inner wood, waiting to awaken. The true hero is the one inside all of us, and such tales stir us partly because of this feeling: that one day our Higher Self will be revealed and justice will be done. Is this why such tales have lingered so long in our imagination?*

TWENTY FOUR

CAPTAIN POUCH

It was early June and the air was golden with seed and sun. Captain Pouch stood astride a haycart, looking down at the protesters gathered before him at Newton. There were hundreds of them – holding their pitchforks and mattocks, scythes and billhooks – men, women and children. Hungry faces, desperate faces; faces of people who hadn't been given much in life, but even that was being taken away from them now.: the right to graze their cattle on common land, gather firewood and grow crops. The lands which had been theirs for generations were being enclosed, parcelled up by the rich landowners.

The people had had enough.

It started in late April, in the Year of Our Lord 1607. Like a wildfire it had spread from Haselbech, Pytchley, and Rushton, crossing the county border into Warwickshire and Leicestershire, until the people broke out in riots. And the firebrand, the figure-head behind all of this stood before them – Captain Pouch! He had quickly become the stuff of legend but here he was in the flesh and blood; scrawny and black-toothed, greasy-haired and bow-legged, but with a fire in him which set them all alight.

'Good people! Hear me! I have the authority from the King and the Lord of Heaven to destroy enclosures and promise to protect all who protest by the contents of my pouch!' He lifted it up, and folk gasped. There it was – his magic pouch. What was in it? Everyone had an idea, but nobody knew. It was the source of constant speculation. But, so far, the luck had been with them. The power of the pouch had protected them.

'Good people! We are not barbarians. We need not use violence in our efforts to destroy the hated enclosures. God is on our side! Right is on our side! By this blessed pouch, I swear it is so.

When an Englishman puts his mind to something, no power on earth can stop him. We fight for our land. Follow me!'

And follow him they did.

It was recorded that three thousand rose in revolt at Hillmorton, Warwickshire, and five thousand at Cotesbach, Leicestershire. They imposed a curfew on the city of Leicester, for it was feared that the good citizens would stream out of the city to join the riots. A gibbet was raised in the city as a warning, but was pulled down by an angry crowd.

Who would have thought that a tinker from Desborough could cause such an upheaval? Not least, John Reynolds himself, as Captain Pouch was originally called. He led his ragged army like a general over the fields of Newton, pulling down hedges and filling ditches. Nothing it seemed could stop them.

Folk had had enough of the Popish Treshams. Their Rushton cousins, with their Triangular Lodge, were the worst. Had not Francis Tresham been involved in the Gunpowder Plot? Not content with trying to blow up Parliament, the Treshams were now seeking to destroy village life with their greedy enclosures, gobbling up field after field. The final straw was the enclosing of the Brand – a section of woodland long a part of Rockingham Forest.

King James himself issued a Proclamation and ordered his dastardly Deputy Lieutenants in Northamptonshire to put down the riots. Women and children were part of the protest, but this did not stop the brutality.

Edward Montagu, one of the Deputy Lieutenants, had spoken against enclosure in Parliament some years earlier, but was now placed by the King in the position effectively of defending the Treshams, with whom there had been a long-running feud. The old Roman Catholic gentry family of the Treshams had long argued with the emerging Puritan gentry family the Montagus of Boughton about territory. Perhaps their rivalry fuelled this revolt as much as anything.

The local armed bands and militia refused the call-up, so the landowners were forced to use their own servants to suppress the rioters. On 8 June 1607 the two sides squared up against each other – those for the Crown, those for the land.

The Royal Proclamation was read twice, but the rioters continued in their actions and the gentry and their forces charged. A pitched battle ensued. The rebels put up a lusty fight – like a badger baited to exhaustion – but eventually the King's men overwhelmed them by force of arms.

Forty to fifty of the rebels were killed that day.

They crushed the Newton Rebellion stone-cold dead. The ringleaders were rounded up, and Captain Pouch was apprehended.

The leaders of the protest were executed in a manner reserved for 'traitors': hanged and quartered.

Seeing their leader swing on the gallows crushed the spirit of the rebellion – the Midland Revolt was over.

John Reynold's pouch was found after he was captured. It was opened – all that was in it was a piece of hard, green cheese.

The Newton Rebellion was one of the last times that the peasantry of England and the gentry were in open conflict. At St Faith's Church in Newton there is a memorial to the men who were executed. Curiously, parish and assize records have disappeared. The Tresham family declined soon after. Ironically, the Montagu family went on through marriage to become the Dukes of Buccleuch, one of the biggest landowners in Britain.

TWENTY-FIVE

BOUDICCA'S LAST STAND

Boudicca surveyed the scene before her with eyes the colour of the wide open sky of her homeland. Her vast army of Celtic warriors rose to life out of the morning mist – mist which snaked in white tendrils along the bend of the valley, slowly burning off in the light of a new day. A day that would decide the fate of Roman Britain. The rising sun, defiantly raising its bronze face, picked out the glint of spear and arm torc, harness and chariot, the spiral tattoos and the woad.

Good men, true men. Her men.

Chieftains and champions, ally tribes of the Iceni, they had risen up to her battle cry, followed her flame-red hair into battle, filled with the righteous anger of a mother's vengeance.

Three cities, for three daughters raped, but still Boudicca's thirst for vengeance was not placated. She would not stop until she had driven the Roman invaders from the land. The warrior queen had become the very embodiment of a downtrodden people, cresting a wave of rage against these metal-hearted men.

It had been an unexpected destiny.

For a while she had been content – hard to conceive it now – as a mother and wife of the chief of the Iceni. Once Prasutagus had been a good man, before he bent his knee to the Invaders; before he became a client king. He said he had done it to protect his people – his first and foremost duty. But what of honour? He was never the same man after that. She had seen it in his eyes. Defeat. When he had died he had hoped to preserve the 'Pax Romana' – compromising, but enduring – by offering the Emperor Nero his kingdom to share with two of his daughters.

But the Emperor does not like to share power.

After the massacre on Mon – when the last of the oak priests were wiped out in their sacred stronghold – it became clear the Romans were intent on more than just subjugation. Their policy clearly changed to one of not just zero tolerance, but virtual geno-cide. They desired to crush every iota of insubordination utterly. They passed a new law: no tribesman could carry weapons beyond those needed for hunting. Even the compliant conquered tribes had to submit. They came and took their prized swords – yanking them from resistant fists. Precious ancestral heirlooms; the phallic power of a people.

That had been hard, but what was to follow was harder. Husbandless, Boudicca found herself defenceless when they came – they flogged her and had Roman slaves rape her daughters in front of her. They let her live, unlike her defiled and brutalised daughters. Better a tame queen who had been taught a harsh lesson in obedience, than a dead one who could become a martyr.

Yet they did not reckon on her fury.

She had pulled herself out of the ashes – her grief had stripped away all sentiment, all kindness. Her sky blue eyes became as cold as steel. In a voice raw with her keening, unequivocal, she had summoned the tribes in war council.

The Goddess had been insulted. There was only one thing to do.

The warhost gathered over several days, swelling in numbers into the hundred thousand. Boudicca watched them arrive with cold satisfaction. Her chariot was prepared. Her war gear gleamed as she led them to battle, her dark cloak flapping behind her. They marched on the Roman cities, destroying them one by one.

Boudicca's army had raised the estuary port of Londinium to the ground, and slaughtered everyone they could find, her warriors consumed by the madness of the red mist. The gore still upon their swords, they moved – slowly, but steadily, an unstoppable behemoth, a massive force encumbered with carts full of supplies and the warriors' families, now lined up on the brow of the hill (so confident were they of battle, they let their wives and children watch) up Watling Street; the irony of using a Roman road not escaping them. By the time they had reached Verulanium – home of the client tribe, the Catuvellauni – they had made the road all but impassable, felling trees and defiling it along the way. The gutless Catuvellauni had the good sense to vacate the place. Boudicca's army found it deserted when they rumbled into town. They wasted no time in putting its buildings to the torch after ransacking it of all its wealth. Before Verulanium and Londinium the same fate had befallen Camulodunum – but there they had caught the citizens off guard, and they put the pensioned legionaries to the sword. It had been their first victory and the most satisfying.

In comfortably plump Camulodunum, Boudicca heard reports of how the citizens had seen the omens of doom: human-shaped cadavers washed in on the ebb tide; dreadful moans heard in the Senate house; the theatre echoed with shrieks; a blood-red stain seen in the sea, and a phantom colony in the estuary in ruins. The womenfolk keened that destruction was at hand, yet the British slaves read the signs differently, keeping their auguries to themselves.

For a while it had seemed as though they could really drive the invaders out. Andraste was with them. Was not her own name synonymous with the goddess of victory?

Had they not put the Ninth Legion to the sword? They had fallen on them like Morrighan from the dark shadows of the wild wood and the tin-hearts had known terror. Two thousand souls had been offered to the thirsty earth.

That was a good day.

But here, this morning, Boudicca felt ... different. All of this bloodshed – where would it get them in the end? All the fallen had once been the children of their mothers. Helpless babies. Sacred life.

Had she become like her enemy, torturing and slaughtering the innocent?

From the folds of her cloak she released a hare and watched closely as it sped across the open plain, jink-jinking this way and that.

For a moment, its fleeting figure seemed to turn into a girl, a young girl dancing ... joined by her sisters. Laughing. Laughing in the sun.

Tears streaked Boudicca's war-paint. In a broken whisper she breathed what she dared not believe: 'My daughters ...' Then a cloud covered the morning sun, and the spell was broken. The single hare darted towards the Roman legion and, caught in a wall of steel, was hacked down. They watched on aghast. Her battle chieftains tried to laugh it off, but Boudicca was grim-faced.

'The dream...'

'Your Majesty?' One of her generals looked on, concerned.

She had dreamed this day, and now she was trapped in the dream. The Icenian Queen watched events unfold around her as though in a nightmare – a powerless victim of greater forces.

The signs were not good, but what could they do? The enemy was upon them. Suetonius had placed ten thousand men in a steep-sided defile before the Celts – the woods behind, an open plain in front – so that they would be forced to meet them on their terms. The dark trees loomed menacingly to the sides. Centurions stood in ranks to the front; light-armed troops waited to the side, and high up on the ridge, the cavalry waited. The centurions raised their banners, clashed their spears upon their shields in a deafening rhythm.

Boudicca's warriors ran bare-chested in front of the enemy, dodging the slingshot and hurling defiance, raising their kirtles to defecate and piss at them.

Many of them rode their magnificent steeds mockingly close to the enemy line. Icenian horses were renowned – in the land there were no finer. But the Legion held rank and did not react to their provocations. They awaited the command of their general.

The air was tense with expectation. The battle was inevitable. This beautiful combe would soon become a slaughter ground.

Boudicca's army hadn't met a Roman legion in the open field of combat yet – the Ninth were defeated in ambush. She knew it wouldn't go well for them, but they were bound by destiny.

If they surrendered now they would be slaughtered anyway. Better to die in honour. If never again such an army rose up against the alien oppressors at least once, it could be sung, the British had resisted. They had shown high and mighty Nero that one remote, damp corner of the Empire would not yield without a fight; that there were some simple savages who valued their land and freedom more than their lives, more than the yoke of so-called civilisation.

'What's that?' one of her men called.

Boudicca turned her fierce stare to the enemy line, as something was tossed into the field before them.

The limp body of the hare lay inert in the grass.

'They insult Andraste!' cried her men, but Boudicca saw something else, beyond the totem of the Goddess. Her own flesh and blood. For her daughters, then.

A mother's love knows no end, even after death.

In her shining war chariot she rode up and down the line of her warriors, meeting their eyes, filling them with her fire. Finally, she called her horses to a halt. They stamped and snorted in the morning light, their harnesses glinting bright. Their queen looked magnificent before them – red hair down to her waist, brightly clad in her finest jewellery; around her neck was a fine golden torc, the sign of her chieftainship. A thick plaid cloak, dyed blue was bound with a brooch of exquisite design. She spoke to her army, her grief-honed voice ringing out over the battlefield: 'Arrogant men think they can conquer the land. They are wrong. The land conquers you. Whatever the outcome of today's battle, the land will win in the end – that is certain.' A roar went up from her army. She waited for it to abate, and then she continued: 'All we can is not disgrace our ancestors. We must face steel with steel, with honour and bravery – in memory of all those slain by the Romans, for all those atrocities they have committed.' Her voice nearly broke, but angry shouts filled the plain, directed at the legions. Boudicca spurred her horses around, finishing with a final provocation: 'Win the battle or perish: that is what I, a woman, will do; you men can live on in slavery if that's what you want. But I fight for this precious land, for our sacred mother, for home!'

She raised her sword and let out an ululation, which was taken up by the black-clad women of the Iceni. Their terrifying voices rose over the meadows, golden in the light of the new day – the sun shone on the dew. It looked beautiful.

Boudicca's army charged, raising their war cry – 'Andraste!'– as the sky darkened with ten thousand javelins hurled towards them.

My daughters, I am coming.

There is some controversy over the site of Boudicca's last battle, but some evidence points to the possibility of two sites in Northamptonshire: Cuttle Mill, Paulersbury; or Church Stowe. This is the description of the battlefield:

Selecting a position in a defile closed in behind by a wood, and having made sure that there was no enemy but in front, where there was an open flat ground unsuited for ambuscades, he drew up his legions in close order, with the light-armed troops on the flanks, while the cavalry was massed at the extremities of the wings. (Tacitus, Ramsay)

In order to level the odds, Suetonius placed his 10,000 men in a defile with woods to his rear and open country without cover in front. When the British attacked they were met by a shower of javelins before the Romans, in close order, pushed forward, beating them down with their shields and killing them with the sword. The British were driven back and their attempts to flee the enclosing wings of cavalry were hampered by the ring of wagons drawn up for their families to see the victory they so confidently expected. Tacitus gives the doubtful figures of 80,000 Britons slain for a cost of 400 Roman dead.

Boudicca apparently poisoned herself, but was buried secretly with great honour in a tomb befitting a Celtic queen by her Roman victors – it remains unfound to this day.

Independent of Boudicca's revolt, rebellions flared up across the country. Eventually the natives were pacified and an uneasy peace settled. Then, in AD 410 the Romans left and their legacy – the villas, the roads, the temples – slowly became obscured by nature, time and man. The Iceni vanished into the wilds of the Fens, their defiant spirit perhaps remaining in the character of the horses and Fensmen.

Whatever the truth, the land conquered all in the end.

Twenty Six

St Patrick
of Banneventa

Patrick had grown up playing in the villa – his parents' house
at Banneventa, just off Watling Street. He had shinned his way
around the hypocausts, when the servants let them cool for their
annual spring clean; he had climbed up onto the red tiled roof and
teetered precariously above the courtyard, seeing the neat farm-
lands stretch out below – rows of tenderly nurtured fruit trees,

ranks of tilled earth, pigs foraging and cattle grazing, the curls of smoke from the bakery and the pottery. It had been a fun place to explore, always an adventure to be had! The dramatic arrivals and departures of citizens on important business, talking with his father – wandering the gardens, deep in discussion, like the philosophers he had been taught about. He had taken to his studies, especially Latin, and loved learning about other countries. One day he hoped to travel, to explore the world. There was so much more out there, beyond the gently undulating fields of Northamptonshire.

Of course, he had known other lands. Had he not been born in Cambria, sixteen years ago, in AD 389? But his father had been given the villa in Banneventa, and so that is where they moved – the Roman official Calpurnius and his British wife, Patrick's mother: a wild, wilful woman, whose British stubborn was the bane of her husband. He could command legions, but not bid his wife do anything she had set her mind against.

But life in the villa was happy enough. It passed in a kind of golden haze – it always seemed to be summer, the fields were always ripe with wheat, swaying gently in a warm breeze. They lived off the fat of the land, and all was well.

They seemed to have everything … but something was lacking, something that made Patrick increasingly restless. The endless seasonal ceremonies were getting tedious. He quickly bored of them. The prayers and offerings to the household gods seemed meaningless to him – they reminded him of a child's toys – and he had outgrown such things.

One day, in a fit of rage – he can't say what triggered it, although he had been growing increasingly irritable as of late – he went to the shrine and smashed up all of the clay figurines, pounding them into dust with a sturdy oak stick.

He was breathing heavily, brow beaded with sweat when they found him, a content look in his eyes, strangely peaceful. His father was informed and strode towards him, dragging with him a dark cloud of anger. Fist clenching, he glowered at the young Patrick. His wife looked aghast at the destruction but pleaded with her husband, clinging to his raised hand. Patrick raised his cheek

– it was what he deserved. No more, no less. But the blow did not come, at least not in the way he expected.

A cry in the distance. Voices. The servants stirred, and a messenger burst into the courtyard. 'The town, the town is burning!'

Patrick's father clenched his jaw, and giving his son a look which said your fate awaits you, my boy, he turned to deal with the disturbance, shrugging away his wife.

His mother looked at him, wide-eyed. 'Run!' Had she lost her wits? She ran about the house, pulling at her hair, carrying out possessions, dropping them, weeping. Servants ran hither and thither. It was chaos.

Patrick pulled a servant's sleeve. 'What is going on?'

The servant looked terrified. 'The Britons are raising Banneventa!'

Patrick seemed to be forgotten in the ensuing chaos. He made his way through the villa and up onto the roof. From there he could see the flames – the whole sky was alight. And out of the red fields – ruddy with a blood harvest – came swathes of marauding warriors, dressed in furs, or naked and tatooed, some sporting animal skins, antlers, leaves – the wild men he had heard his father talk of when he thought he was out of earshot. The strangers over the border. The Waleas, the Pictoi, the Celts.

He saw his father gather his men, ready to defend the villa. He saw him ride out to meet them, unsheathing his sword, into the field of fire. And that was the last he saw of him.

Screams of his mother split the sky.

Then the warriors were in the villa, knocking over trellises, grabbing maidservants, pitchers of wine, curing hams, anything that shone. They cut down any servant foolish enough to stand in their way, and sometimes more, for good measure. What happened to his mother, he didn't see, but soon a pile of bodies littered the courtyard. A terracotta tile slipped, dislodged by his foot, and smashed on a barbarian's shaggy head. The beast-man looked up, snarled a black-toothed smile, pulled his axe from the skull of an old retainer and came after him.

Patrick, cornered on the roof, leapt as he had seen the wild deer leap gates. As the beast-man appeared, a little breathless, he jumped

– slipping from his grasp – over the villa wall, and rolled onto the boggy grass beyond.

The breath was knocked out of him but he lived. His young body sprang back like a sapling. Heart pounding, he darted through the long grass – and for a moment it felt like he would make the trees. He would escape the massacre. What then, who knows, but he was free.

Then the two warriors emerged from the undergrowth – camouflaged against the land, as though they were a part of it. They blocked his way with their spears. One butted him and Patrick spun with the impact; a flash of burning villa, the glare of flames and the cool darkness of the trees. He fell into the green, and all was black.

What happened next Patrick only remembers in snatches: being man-handled into a cart, chained with others; a long bumpy ride to the coast, his first glimpse of the grey sea; a stinking hold, retching until raw to the motion of the waves, feeling like he wanted to die; cold and shivering on some quayside – strange red-haired people poking and prodding him; the clink of coin, spit and a handshake; freed from his rusty manacles at last, but bound with rope and led over the hills and far away.

Patrick heard the lowing of a cow; the cluck of hens in a yard; the gabble of geese; water spurting from a pump; the singing of a maid as she went about her chores ... Was he ... was he back home? Maybe it had all been a bad dream. 'Mother?' he called out tentatively, his voice cracking. No reply. 'Father?' The door burst open, blinding him, and a pail of cold water was thrown over him, making him gasp with shock.

'Get up,' spoke a hard voice. 'You have to earn your keep here, lad. No shirkers. Everyone pulls their weight.'

Slowly, over the coming days, Patrick learnt he was in Erin – he had been taken slave by the marauders and sold to an Irish landowner. Here he was forced into a miserable life as a cattle-minder. Day after day of relentless drudgery – sleeping on a rough sack; eating gruel and weevil-riddled bread; endless wind and rain; hills as hard as the faces, staring blankly back at him – treating him like some kind of idiot, because he could hardly catch their strange turns of phrase, weird words, and odd lilt. Yet, he was bright and picked up vocabulary as some picked up windfall apples. Soon he knew not only the basics to get by in this cruel life, but more than he let on; eavesdropping on conversations while playing mute. Soon, he learnt the lay of the land – devising a mental map of the area in his head. He planned and prepared, hiding away scraps of food, and saving rags of clothing in readiness.

Patrick learnt to almost love that land, minding the cattle every day, high up on their summer pasture. He had been given increasingly free rein – proving he was a 'tame slave', and a dim one at that. They knew he would not roam far before his belly brought him back. He always seemed to eat more than his little frame needed. There was a hunger inside of him, no doubt. But not a hunger they knew.

A hungry fire that would one day set them all alight.

As he minded his cattle he realised there must be something more. Surely humans were not just dumb animals, content to graze in the fields; their fates dictated by the whims of others? A cruel stick or a kind word; a milkmaid's hands or a butcher's knife. The servants and their masters had their own ways of lightening the yoke that life placed around their necks – with a beaker of strong cider, a jig on a fiddle, a merry dance about the fire, or an outlandish tale late at night. Sometimes, Patrick caught them praying to wild pagan gods, which minded him of his family's household pantheon. A posy of flowers left by a spring, a saucer of cream by the backdoor, a charm of herbs in the rafters. But this was not enough for Patrick either. He saw through it, he saw through it all – until it felt as though his brain would split open.

There. Had. To. Be. Another. Way.

Then, a rumble in the sky above, the dark clouds like an angry scowl. No, not the sky, the mountain – the mountain was falling on him. An avalanche!

Patrick watched, hypnotised, as a boulder rolled towards him. He was paralysed. There was nothing he could do. It was too late. Then, just before the boulder rolled him into oblivion, a lightning bolt split it asunder and the two shards passed either side of him.

Patrick opened his eyes. He lived. He looked down the hillside at the shattered shards which had missed him by inches, then at the sky above, where broiling clouds now parted to reveal a gleam of light.

Suddenly, he knew what he must do. He had been saved for a reason. He had work to do, the work of the one true God.

Filled with fire, he gathered his hidden stash of food and clothing, and set off, into a hidden pass – not turning to look back at the land that had been his prison until now.

He slipped through the pass and was long gone before they noticed he was missing. Filled with an inexhaustible energy, he felt he could keep going for hours, miles, days. And he did, making it to the coast and negotiating his way onto a boat, using his gall and his wits to secure a passage to Gaul.

He looked back at the green line of coast, diminishing in the ship's wake. He would return. There was much work to do.

A decade later, a young man walked amid the ruins of Banneventa – lingering as he passed amongst the outline of the old villa, long fallen to ruin and reclaimed by the wild. He had a pilgrim's staff and looked like he had spent many days on the road. He was lean and wiry, and filled with a hungry fire.

Kneeling, he pulled back the undergrowth to reveal the fragments of a household shrine. There, amid the weeds, he could make out a figurine of some heathen god. A tear forming on his cheek, he reached out a trembling hand to touch it – just as an adder uncoiled from its slumber amongst the broken shards, hissing a forked tongue at this intruder in its lair. Patrick cried out, leapt up in alarm and disgust and brought his staff down upon it, again and again.

Composing himself, he looked out over the land. He would plough the Devil out of this soil and plant the true Vine of Christ.

And, when he had finished here, he would venture into the West – to an emerald isle where the pagan Irish waited – rich soil, waiting to be ploughed.

Patrick grabbed a handful of the rich Northamptonshire loam. He inspected it – scrutinising a worm which wriggled free of the sod. Yes, there was much work to do.

In 432, Patrick returned to Erin, where his miracles and piety convinced the people of the truth of his message. He died in around 461 and became the patron saint of Ireland.

As a child I played in an excavation of a Roman villa near to my grandparents' house in Briar Hill – running around the trenches, on the same level as Patrick would have been.

TWENTY SEVEN

THE SAINT
AND THE GEESE

Saint Werburga – patron saint of women and children – was the daughter of Ermenilda (who would become a saint as well) and Wulfhere, ruler of the Anglo-Saxon kingdom of Mercia in the seventh century.

From an early age, Werburga showed a strong desire for the religious life, rather than her father's worldly court. Her father was the first Saxon king to be baptised. Before he died in 675 he did much to spread his faith throughout Mercia.

When the time was right, Werburga took the veil and entered a convent at Ely. Here, her piety and organising ability were quickly recognised, and she rose to the rank of Mother Superior. She served as a Mother Superior of many convents, before becoming Chief Abbess of all Mercia – a powerful woman of her day.

Saint Werburga (as she eventually became known) spent several years at Weedon Abbey. Here, a miracle that would confirm her great sanctity occurred.

One day, a huge gaggle of wild geese suddenly swooped down from the sky and settled in the surrounding fields and orchards. The villagers tried to frighten them away, but the birds ignored their efforts and began to devour the fruit and crops. Nothing could escape their deadly beaks. Their honking became a clamour, haranguing the good citizens day and night. The sound of the geese became the sound of terror to the villagers. 'The geese! The geese have us surrounded! We're doomed!' they cried. In despair, the villagers went to Werburga to beg her help.

As soon as she heard of their plight, she ordered several of her servants to round up the geese and bring them into the abbey. Amazingly, the birds at once became docile and converged on the abbey of their own free will, allowing themselves to be penned up.

The next morning, Werburga went to the yard and admonished the geese for their misdeeds. The flock stood there and received their admonishment in silence. They lowered their beaks in shame. One let out a disconsolate honk. After she had finished scolding them, it is said that they stretched their necks forward, begging forgiveness and promising – in their goose-like way – not to cause further mischief.

Werburga then allowed them to fly away.

Soon afterwards, however, the geese returned.

They had discovered that one of their flock had been missing since their visit to the abbey – and accused the abbey servants of killing and eating one of their gaggle in the night.

Werburga was aggrieved that her trust had been betrayed, and promised to punish those responsible for the crime. Then she ordered the bones of the dead bird to be brought to her.

Once this was done, bidding the geese farewell, she asked the chief gander to count his flock as it flew away. He did so, and found that the number was once again complete.

The missing bird had been miraculously restored to life!

And from that point Werburga's own legend took flight. Living a long and devout life she would gather in the faithful flock – and the wild goose of the Holy Spirit would soar through her.

Werburga died in about the year 700 at a nunnery at Threeckingham in Lincolnshire, and her body is said to have resisted decay for nearly 200 years. It finally crumbled to dust in 875, when the Danes invaded England. Her remains were then taken to Chester where the Mercian Princess Ethelfleda built a convent to house them. During times of danger the monks of Chester carried her shrine around the city walls and once, in 1180, the city is alleged to have been saved from fire by this ritual.

THE BEAST OF NINE CHURCHES

Church Stowe, just off Watling Street, a stone's throw from Daventry, is one of the gems of the county. An inordinately pretty spot, with its dramatic hillside location and sweeping views of wooded wolds, it feels dropped in from another part of England. There seems no unlikelier spot for a tale of supernatural monsters and awkward architecture, but that is what those ne'er-do-well storytellers want us to believe. Suspend your disbelief and listen, as I tell you the tale of the Beast of Church Stowe.

A good few centuries ago, before Billy the Conqueror came a-marching in, the good folk of the ancient settlement of Church Stowe decided they wanted to build a church dedicated to Archangel Michael. Now, these were hairy Saxons (despite the condition of their souls) so you might have to forgive them for their simple behaviour – as you'll see.

Anyway, the builders set about locating a suitable spot for their stone temple. They paced up and down, casting about with their sighting poles, scratching their tonsured heads. They settled on a nice spot – a level bit of ground down in the valley, where the stream winds by, merrily chuckling to itself, as though it knows a joke that we do not.

Trenches were dug and masonry was manhandled. Things were off to a good start and the builders downed their tools to go off and slake their thirst in the nearby mead hall, as builders have been wont to do for centuries. A flaxen, buxom barmaid was no doubt waiting to serve them tankards of foaming ale or the like. Ah, the good life!

Anyway, where was I? Oh yes. The next day they returned to discover to their dismay all their hard work gone awry – literally. The tools, trenches and masonry had been cast up the hillside.

What was the world coming to, hey, when a worker can't leave his tools lying around? Or the foundations of a church?

But these were good Christian Saxons, so they turned the other cheek, and, locating a slightly better spot – for their first choice perhaps wasn't their best in the cold light of day – they set to laying the foundations once more.

Come the end of the day, they rubbed their chins and look on with pride. Satisfied that this was by far the better spot after all, the men went back to the mead hall.

Alas and shock, the same sight greeted them the next morning. The tools, trenchboards and stones, all scattered even further up the hillside. Sighing at such vandalry they chose another site and went back to work.

Alas, the same thing happened a third day, a fourth, fifth, sixth, seventh and eighth. Finally, enough was enough.

They decided to do something about. At last, I hear you cry! A man was selected by lots, who turned out to be the youngest monk among them. He was made to stay up all night and keep a watch on their eighth building site.

And so the young monk found himself in the middle of the night, wrapped up in the dark, with only a guttering torch for company, trembling not so much from the cold, but from the thought of what he might see.

Sure enough, in the dead of night, just as he was nodding off, a great commotion could be heard. Nervously, the wide-eyed monk took the torch and inspected the site. His hands grew sweaty and his bony knees knocked together as he approached the disturbance. 'In the Lord's name, who are you?'

Thrusting his torch forward, the monk was astonished by two large lambent eyes looking back at him. There was a snort, and then the thing continued. Asking for God's protection, the monk nervously inspected the critter. It was no bigger than a hog but just as hairy, and possessed with an incredible strength for its size, tossing the masonry like apples.

The monk dropped his torch on the floor and fled.

Pale-faced and still trembling, the young monk related what he had beheld the next day, amid the scattered stones, tools and planks, which were even nearer to the hilltop.

The builders consulted and decided that some devilry was at work, which they had better not mess with. In this instance, circumspection was the best possible solution. They built their church on the brow of the hill, well away from the devil's playground below.

They nervously awaited the outcome of their handiwork, but to their delight they discovered the site intact the next morrow. And the following morning. When, after a whole week, it still remained undisturbed they took it as a sign that the bad spirits of place – whatever they were – were finally happy.

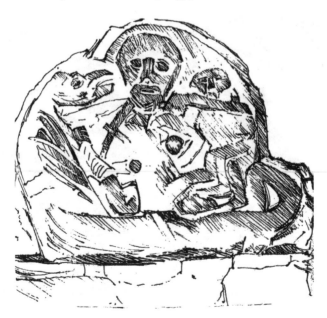

And so they finished building their church, on its ninth site, and that is where it stands to this day as the Church of St Michael. To this day, the name of the parish is Stowe Nine Churches.

When they had finished and consecrated their church, a dark stranger passed by, wielding a crooked staff and wearing a crooked hat. Through crooked teeth he whispered to the young monk, almost below hearing, that, 'The People of Peace are pleased with yer handiwork. Afore, they were most upset when you had tried to build upon their dancing ground – as anyone would be! They tried to hint at where it should go, and they's were glad when ye finally got the message. Nine times lucky. Yer stone god box will stand its ground, with their blessing.' And with that mysterious missive, the crooked stranger scurried off with remarkable speed around the corner. The monk called after him and gave chase, wanting to ask him many questions, but he could find no sign of him. He had vanished into thin air. The monk rubbed his eyes – looking down the vale, he thought he saw eight phantom churches in different locations before they merged into the one on the hill.

Such siting legends are not uncommon – there are several in the county (often involving wandering stonework, the stone eagles on the gatepost of Drayton House at Lowick, or the Stone Moses at Weekly and Warkton) and countless numbers across Britain. Are they evidence of some kind of geomantic 'conflict'? The disturbance of genius loci by insensitive masons? The imposition of Christian temples on pagan sites? The displacement of chthonic practices by subsequent cultures? In Oriental cultures, the problem would have been avoided by the consultation of a Feng Shui expert, many of whom are employed to this day in the siting of new buildings and the harmonising of old ones. Whatever the reason, to this day the village sign ambivalently states::

   'Church Stowe
   Stowe Nine Churches'

TWENTY NINE

THE ANGEL
AND THE CROSS

Do you know where the centre of England is? This has been a matter of debate and dispute for centuries, but the matter can be finally settled thanks to divine intervention.

It began far from England, in the heat and dust of the Holy Land. The weary pilgrim placed down his staff and sat down by the side of the rubble-strewn road and rubbed his sore feet. His shoes, made by his own fair hands – like father, like son, he had carried on his family's trade – had served him well, carrying him across Europe and into the Middle East, along long perilous trails – braving wildwood, bandit, war, tricksters and pedlars of false grails.

Taking off his hat, sporting the scallop-shell of the pilgrim, he fanned himself with it – it was so hot here, so bright. Coming from a softer, damper land, he had still not got used to it. Squinting, he looked up at the city before him, the various temples and spires competing for dominance. Bells rang out over the hustle and bustle of thousands of people coming and going through its gates. It was the eight century of Our Lord, and he had made it to Jerusalem. His soul was surely saved by this pious act. And he needed salvation. His soul was in a poorer condition than his poor old feet.

He acted the penniless and penitent pilgrim here, but back home he was a man of power, of influence. He had been cruel, yes, and vain. He had acquired wealth for himself in countless dubious ways. His coffers were full but his heart was empty. All of those glittering coins and trinkets had left him unfulfilled.

There had to be something more.

And that is when, one day, walking amid the noisome stalls of Sheep Street, he had an idea. He would go on pilgrimage to the Holy Land, to purge himself of his sins.

The pilgrim lined up and entered through one of the gates, under the stern eyes of the guards, and then he was in! Jerusalem, in all its glory, opened up before him. He stopped and stared; only to be elbowed out of the way, making him step in the gutter. Yet he was so euphoric from the ardours of his journey that he didn't care. He had made it. He looked around, grinning like a moon-touched loon. The narrow streets were full of noise and colour – the cries of trinket sellers, icon hawkers, fortune tellers, farmers with their produce arrayed before them – such exotic wares, the likes of which he had never seen before. With the last of his coins he purchased a large, succulent looking fruit and held it to his nose, savouring its smell. It was enough to make him salivate. The pilgrim imagined its cool juice, running down his throat, assuaging his burning thirst.

But, just before he sank his teeth into it, another passer-by bumped into him, making him drop it. The pilgrim cursed under his breath, casting the stranger an evil stare – but it was too late, the perpetrator was lost in the crowd, and his fruit was rolling away from him.

Quickly, he pursued it as it rolled down the alleyways, away from the main crowds. Soon he was lost in a maze of passageways – perfect for thieves – but he could only think about his wayward fruit.

He would not let it go! He had come so far, endured such adversity – he would not let such a simple thing thwart him.

The fruit occasionally caught the odd dusty beam of light which penetrated the maze.

Nearly … within … reach.

The pilgrim lunged, just as the fruit rolled down a gap between two tumble-down buildings.

Cursing he knelt down and peered in. Luck! The object of his desire had got stuck against something blocking the narrow gap. The place smelt foetid, but he had to get that fruit. Gingerly, he stuck in his arm and, straining, reached for it. Something scuttled over his naked arm. A large black rat darted out of the gap and along the edge of the buildings! He quickly pulled out his arm, rubbed it vigorously. Then, composing himself, he tried again. Nearly ... nearly ... there! He had his hand around it and triumphantly pulled it out. He rubbed it free of filth and sank his teeth into it with a satisfied sigh. For a while he was lost in the pleasure of the taste – sharp but refreshing. Then, wiping his mouth, he peered into the gap out of curiosity. What was it that had blocked it?

There, he could see it now. An old stone cross – wedged in between the buildings. How odd. Perhaps it might be worth something.

Maybe his fortune had changed.

Laughing, he reached in and strained and strained until his fingernails scraped the stone. Slowly, painfully, he worked it towards his grasp – there, he had it! Making sure no one was around, he carefully pulled it out and, dusting it free of cobwebs, he inspected it.

It was a stone cross of simple design. It felt old, very old. As he ran his fingers over it, the hairs on the back of his neck stood on end. He felt like he was being watched.

A strange light and a warmth filled the darkened alleyway.

The pilgrim slowly turned and beheld before him a dazzling figure, glowing in rainbow colours – overlapping planes of light like a stained-glass window in a cathedral.

The being spoke to him in a voice warm and enfolding.

'Take this cross and bury it in the very heart of your homeland.'
'Where?'

'The precise centre. The golden cross. Do so, and all will be well.'

The vision faded and the pilgrim was left shaking. What had he seen? Perhaps there had been something wrong with that fruit. Afeared, he threw the pulpy core away. The stone cross was solid enough in his hand. That felt real.

Heart pounding, he got up.

Wrapping it in a rag, he placed the cross in his satchel and made his way quickly along the alleyway – walking with increasing purpose.

The pilgrim beheld his old home town with a sigh of relief. The journey back had been hard. Many times he had come close to losing his sacred relic, but he had held onto it for dear life amid the stormy crossings and dark nights. And now he was home finally, and he wept at the sight of Hamtun. Humble as it was, it was his home, and he was overcome with emotion at seeing it again. There were times when it looked as though he never would. But something had driven him. The words of an angel – yes, that is what it was. He knew that now. He had not told a soul – he did not want to risk the magic leaking away in the cold light of day. This had happened to him for a reason, and it was *his* sacred duty.

He went to St Peter's to pray in gratitude for his safe return. As he knelt there, the Holy Spirit descended and told him precisely where he must bury the cross. At the crossroads of Gold Street and Horsemarket Street … the golden cross!

A man on fire, he set about his task with fervour.

In the middle of the night, when not a soul was in sight, he took his spade and dug. The spirit guided him – here, here was the very centre of Hamtun, the very centre of England itself.

Who would have thought it? The bottom of Gold Street – the heart of the land! Every day, countless folk criss-crossed it unknowing that they trod on sacred soil. The cross was buried deep, the hole filled in, the soil patted down, so that not a mark, not a trace, would reveal its whereabouts. With a contented sigh, the man finally felt at peace. He stood by the crossroads and watched the world go by, and smiled.

With thanks to my fellow Northamptonian, the now London-based actor Robert Goodman, who first told me about this over a cup of tea in the capital. At the Gold Street crossroads there now stands a massive multiplex leisure complex called 'Sol Central' – a mundane monument to the centre of England. Is the stone cross still there? Certainly, nearby is a church built by the Knights Templar (the Church of the Holy Sepulchre) so who knows what was brought back from the Crusades to the town?

THIRTY

THE
BLESSED STREAM

Becket rode away from Northampton under a cloud. Witchcraft, can you believe it! To be accused of such foolery, and he, an Archbishop! That infernal King – blast him! He had fled the castle via the postern gate disguised as a friar. Pausing only briefly to slake his thirst at a spring on the edge of town, he had ridden throughout the following day, and by evening he reached Stony Stratford, both rider and horse in need of rest.

Becket asked a passing labourer where he might find shelter for the night. The man pointed up the road. 'There's a monastery at Deanshanger, your reverence – only two miles yonder.'

Becket thanked the man and carried on. When he arrived at the monastery, he wasn't recognised. They took in their brother and gave him a simple cell and lodging.

Becket gratefully accepted their hospitality. Once his horse was seen to, he washed and retired for the night.

In the middle of the night, the monastery was stirred from its quietude by a loud knocking. Who the Devil could it be at this hour? The monks gathered to find out – it was the man from the road, a labourer, begging to see their very reverend guest.

What was he blathering on about?

The labourer scanned the robed and tonsured monks, their serious, pious faces illuminated by torches. To their astonishment he pointed, identifying their guest as the Archbishop. Was he out of

his wits? No. Becket stepped forward and revealed his true identity, showing his seal of office.

Becket was impressed by the labourer who had identified him when all the monks had not. He asked what he could do for the man.

'Well,' the farmhand explained, wringing his hands, 'it's such a humble task for one such as yourself I feel a fool to ask it.'

Becket encouraged him. 'Go on.'

The man cleared his throat. 'It's our brook see. Been tainted. Wondered if you could … '

'Turn it to wine?' Becket joked, and the monks chortled. The man coloured. 'No, I thought not. Forgive my jest. I can bless it for you, if you think that will help? In return for the help you gave me on the road. Show me on the morrow, but for now, avail yourself of these good monks' hospitality.'

The next day the man led the Archbishop to the stream at Deanshanger. Sure enough, a noisome reek was issuing from it.

Becket knelt on the sward and bowed his head in prayer.

The labourer bowed his head and kept his eyes shut tight, though he couldn't help but sneak a glance. He saw Becket sign a cross over the stream with his fingers.

'There. God be with you.'

The farmhand thanked the Archbishop, who rode off.

After he had watched Becket ride into the distance, the man turned to look down at the stream. 'Well, bless my soul!' It sparkled with a crystal clear clarity.

Thomas Becket was murdered in Canterbury Cathedral, 29 December 1170. He was canonised two years later. He was tried in Northampton Castle in 1164, of which only the postern gate survives. St Thomas's Hospital and Becket's Well in Becket's Park, where he was believed to have stopped to drink, commemorate him. The scene in the castle is dramatised in Shakespeare's King John.

THIRTY ONE

THE CHALICE
AND THE HEART

In the 1550s it was hard being Catholic in England. John Styles, the vicar of St Mary's Church at Woodford, lost his parish because of his beliefs. He fled to a monastery in Belgium, taking with him a costly chalice from the church – his most precious relic.

Perhaps it had broken his heart to flee his homeland, and to see his fellow Catholics persecuted so, for soon afterwards he died there.

Several years passed. Styles' treasure seemed lost to history, but then Andrew Powlet brought the chalice, together with John's heart, back to Woodford, where he was appointed the new vicar. Alas, with the passage of time, both relics were mislaid and forgotten.

In 1862, Powlet's ghost was seen in the hallway of Woodford Rectory by the young man who then had the living. It appeared twice, each time hovering near a certain panel in the wall. Examination revealed a secret cavity which contained the missing chalice and a faded letter. The letter led to the discovery of John's heart, entombed in a pillar in the church.

The heart is still there, and can be seen through a glass panel in the pillar.

THIRTY-TWO

THE
DRUMMER BOY

On dark moonlit nights he can be heard, by those foolish enough to wander Fermyn Woods at such an ungodly hour. The Drummer Boy, there he goes – can you not hear it above the pounding of your heart? A ghostly rat-a-tat-tat, echoing through the lonely glades of Cat's Head Hill.

His is a sad tale. It relates back to the time the Black Watch mutinied. The Black Jocks, the Ladies from Hell, the Forty Twa; they were called many things, but not to their faces. Their dark tartan was the bane of the Highland. Some say it reflected their black hearts.

Whatever it was that provoked them, they took their motto to heart: *Nemo me impune lacessit* – no one provokes me with impunity.

In 1743, they were ordered to London for an inspection by King George II. But on the long march south, rumours flew that they were to be shipped to the West Indies to fight in the War of Austrian Succession, or some other fool's conflict. When they arrived in London, after many days' steady marching, they were spurned by the Monarch. This contempt was the last straw. Many of them left in disgust to make their way back home, some taking a route through the county.

Soldiers without discipline can be dangerous. Some said they raised hell, getting raucously drunk every night, getting into fights, thieving, and tumbling the local women. And accompanying them every step of the way, the rat-a-tat-tat of the drummer boy, who watched on dumbly as the men caused havoc. He knew it was wisest to keep mum; let his drum be his tongue. There was a time when being their drummer boy felt like an honour, keeping the beat as they marched in rhythm to glory: playing 'Hielan' Laddie' when they marched quick; 'My Home' when slow. But now, his drumsticks felt like lead, and his playing became the erratic ticking of a broken clock.

Enough! The worthies cried. This will not be tolerated.

Captain Bell of Dingley was summoned to apprehend them in the vicinity of Fermyn Woods.

There was a skirmish. Cries of men. The ring of steel on steel. Blood and bodies falling onto the forest floor. The Black Watch were routed and fled into the trees, only to be hunted down like dogs. No one was spared.

The drummer boy had stood by, watching in wide-eyed silence. He banged his drum louder and louder at the slaughter before him – 'Hielan' Laddie, Hielan' Laddie, Hielan' Laddie' – until one of the militia turned on him. 'Silence!' he shouted, cutting the boy down with a single blow.

The drum rolled to a stop against a tree. His sticks landed in the mulch. And his broken form lay still as his bright young blood seeped into the soil of Cat's Head Wood.

For many years afterwards, a small boy could be seen dancing on the mound, playing his drum.

Fermyn Woods is now a popular country park with a splendid playground and cafe. It is hard to imagine this place being the scene of dark doings – a conspiracy against the Crown and the murder of an innocent drummer boy, whose ghost is said to haunt the area of Cat's Head Hill.

Another ghostly drummer is said to be seen at Drummer's Mound, near Barford Bridge, between Kettering and Corby. In Sudborough, a grassy mound by the side of Lady Wood is known locally as the Soldier's Grave. At dusk, the ghostly form of a Scottish piper, wearing a long dark mantle, is seen on the mound, playing a mournful tune. The Black Watch was recaptured, three of the leaders were shot in the Tower of London, and the remainder of the regiment were shipped to Flanders.

THE STRANGE FOREST

THE STAG'S HEAD

Foresters were once very unpopular – the warders of the wood were often cruel and corrupt. Was this in the job description? Or did it just attract a certain sort of ruffian?

One such fellow was Matthew of Thurlbear. He was patrolling an area of Beanfield Lawn in Rockingham forest (by its very name suggesting a former common) with his brother, James, and other foresters, when they were alerted to the presence of five poachers with greyhounds (one was of a distinctive, tawny colour) chasing deer, bold as brass in broad daylight!

The poachers saw the foresters coming and stood their ground, shooting arrows in their direction. Two arrows struck Matthew, one striking him a mortal blow. The poachers fled into 'the thickness of the wood' and escaped.

Three weeks later, James (still mourning the loss of his brother) was invited to dine with the abbot of Pipewell Abbey. Perhaps the abbot felt some sympathy to the young man in his time of distress.

As James arrived at the abbey and dismounted he saw a greyhound with a distinctive, unusual tawny colouring – the same one that had been with the poachers who had killed his brother. The hound belonged to Simon of Kilsworthy, a guest of the abbot.

James identified the felon, who was subsequently taken into custody at Northampton. Justice, it seemed, was served.

But the story continues. Two years later it was alleged that James was frequently seen 'assembling eighteen armed men in all the bailwicks, to wreak destruction to the venison of the lord king'. A gamekeeper-turned-poacher. Had his grief turned his mind to vengeance? Or was he on the ultimate stag night?

In connection to this fragment of forest lore, it was recorded in Rockingham Forest that a sinister 'magical' rite took place at Bullax Wood near Lowick in 1255. The antlered head of a buck was stuck on a spindle – a version of the stang or pole used in witchcraft – like a menacing two-fingered snub against authority and a souvenir of the poachers' activities: 'On a stake in the middle of a clearing which is called Harleruling, placing in the mouth of the aforesaid head a certain spindle and made the mouth gape towards the sun, in great contempt of the lord king and of his foresters.' The forest officials, after 'raising the hue', gave chase but were further humiliated by a shower of arrows aimed at them and had to flee, unable to resist the onslaught. All the poachers were eventually caught, except two who failed to appear at court and were declared outlaws.

THE WILD HUNTSMAN OF WHITTLEBURY

Let me tell you a tragic tale of woodland lust.

It is easy to imagine the dark groves of Whittlebury Forest being entangled with bloody deeds and a spectral huntsman. A walk there is enough to stir anyone's imagination.

Journey back down the taproot of time now, and imagine eavesdropping upon this green scene from yesteryear.

It was a warm and sunny spring day; a day when the very earth shouts for joy. Who cannot be stirred by amorous feelings – if only for the life itself – at such times?

Such was the case when a member of a visiting Royal hunting party bespied a beautiful daughter of a forester – her long tawny hair tumbling over her shoulders as she bent to pick early flowers, singing to herself. He fell in love with her there and then, or so he fooled himself. He simply had to have her.

'What a pretty posy of flowers,' the noble huntsman whimsied. 'How much would you like for them?'

The forester's daughter gave the man an appraising glance, noticing how his gaze seemed more on her bosom than her posy. 'They are not for sale,' she said, head held high.

'Priceless, indeed,' he observed warmly. He liked this girl. She had pluck.

As she walked on by, tossing her hair, he turned his horse and slowly followed her, making small talk, trying to find a chink in her armour of amour. The forester's daughter was not unflattered by the attention, and as she made her way to her father's cottage, a sly smile broke out on her face.

When the forester's daughter walked out the next day, she found a bouquet of flowers waiting for her. She inspected it appraisingly. There was no message upon it, but it did not take a genius to work out where it had come from.

The next day, a basket of fruit was on her doorstep, and on the third day, a fine dress wrapped in a parcel.

Slowly, her heart warmed to the dedicated huntsman. So when she 'happened' to bump into him, she gave him the time of day.

She lingered a little and made sweet talk like the cooing of a dove. He amused her. With a glance, a smile, a stroke of a strand, she led him on a merry dance.

As a puppet on a string, she dandled him. She enjoyed the feeling of power it gave her. The man was a fool, a rich fool.

When he invited her to see a particular 'bird's nest' she agreed to meet him there, but failed to show, sniggering from the shadows.

She placated his irritation with soft words; a hand gently placed upon his, and even allowed him to brush his rough lips against her smooth cheek.

Finally, she agreed to meet him in Marion's Bower – a well-known wooing place – for a picnic on the morrow. When she failed to show, the huntsman (who was dressed in ridiculous attire – velvets and silks, with an outlandish wig and brightly buttoned coat, pacing up and down like a preening peacock) was beside himself. He took to drinking the wine he had brought along, and soon finished the bottle.

In a drunken rage, he rode his horse hard through the woods, calling out her name. The forester's daughter hid in the shade; both thrilled and afeared by the effect she had caused.

Suddenly, the huntsman cried out – he had ridden straight into a jagged branch and his head spun in the air, surprised at finding itself detached from his body.

The forester's daughter fled in terror. What had she done?

Days passed and it was as though the wood held its breath. The forester's daughter stayed in her room, refusing to eat. She looked as pale as death and her father worried dreadfully about her.

Then, on a moonlit night, a spectral whinnying and snorting could be heard – or was it the wild wind howling through the trees? Something, or someone, was outside – a skeletal branch scratched at the leaded window of her room, but she dare not look.

Then, beside herself – after many sleepless nights – the forester's daughter wandered to the spot where they had first met, flowers tangled in her hair, wearing only her long white night dress. There was a snort and a stamp from the shadows and a black horse appeared, bearing the headless form of the huntsman. With him, a pack of spectral hounds, eyes glowing in the dark.

Screaming, the forester's daughter fled into the woods, like a deer in terror of its life, pursued by the headless spectre and his pack of phantom hounds. After they had caught her and cornered her, the hounds tore her apart. Silence descended on the grove. Blood and flowers mingle with the leaves.

Like a deadly rite of spring, the grisly scene is re-enacted every year. Anyone witnessing the dreadful scene will be doomed to meet a nasty end within the year, so watch out as you walk the groves of Whittlebury.

In a county of once substantial woodland, legends of ghostly huntsmen and poachers are unsurprisingly prolific. In Historical Legends of Northamptonshire *(1880) Alfred T. Story describes the huntsmen: 'In their quaint dresses of Lincoln green dashing across the glades on fiery steeds cheering their hell hounds with unearthly glee.' Charles Montagu-Douglas-Scott set the legend in ballad form as 'The Wild Huntsman of Whittlebury':*

> *Ho, ho! For the Whittlebury's huntsman true*
> *The huntsman who hunts by the keen moonlight!*
> *Hurrah! For his hounds that a maid pursue!*
> *She crosses a moonlit ride in view,*
> *Tallyho! And a scream that startles the night,*
> *Forever, and aye when the moon is bright.*

Thirty-Four

The Monk's Revenge

Rockingham Castle stands tall, grey and proud on a hill overlooking the Welland Valley. Picturesque as it is now, the stronghold built for William the Conqueror at Rockingham and replaced by the present castle in 1547, was the scene of a tragedy long ago, one that has become enshrined in the legends of the castle.

It was a crisp autumnal day. Young Lord Zouch of Rockingham was out hunting with his friend, Lord Neville. As they galloped along, they talked and laughed, as carefree as two lords should be – the world at their feet. What could topple them from their high horses?

They paused at a stream to let their steeds slake their thirst, while they did the same. It was here that Lord Neville, checking no one else was in earshot, broke some shocking news to his friend – Lady Zouch had a lover.

The silence was terrible as the news sank in.

'Lord Zouch?' his friend called out, concerned, but Zouch was beside himself with rage. As Zouch galloped off, his friend watched him go with a wry smile.

In a purple temper, Lord Zouch rode back home as fast as his horse could carry him. He mounted the stairs with swift, silent strides, and burst open the heavy door of their bedchamber. There he was greeted with a sight which turned his blood to lava – a monk with his wife!

His wife, pale as a sheet, implored her husband to lower his sword; to let her explain. But Zouch was deaf to her imprecations. In a blind fury he plunged his sword into the robed figure. Lady Zouch screamed and fainted.

The Lord, grimly satisfied, pulled back the hood of the devil who had seduced his wife. Now it was his turn to go pale. For before him, prone on the floor in a widening pool of blood, was his own sister, Clara.

When his wife revived she saw Zouch weeping by the cold body of his sister.

'She ... she was meant to be in a nunnery,' he kept saying, shaking his head in disbelief.

The tableaux seemed to freeze. Time slowed as they watched the dark blood inch its way across the floor.

Hollowly, his wife explained to him that Clara had left her nunnery in disguise to meet a monk she loved.

Zouch mouthed 'monk' like it was a stone. 'But I was told you had ... had taken a lover ...' he muttered.

'Who told you this lie?' cried out Lady Zouch.

'Lord Neville,' was his reply, his mouth dry, the words bitter.

'Neville! Curse his name! His "friendly" warning sprang from hatred and jealousy, and you know why? Because I, your loyal wife, had rejected his loathsome advances. He did this to get back at me.'

Zouch gritted his teeth and clenched his fists.

He stormed out of the room under a dark cloud, and nothing his wife could say would stop him.

However, bent on revenge as he was, as Lord Zouch was about to ride in pursuit of Neville, a monk stopped him.

'Who are you? Another devil in disguise?'

The monk pulled back his hood to reveal a handsome young man, tears streaking his face.

'I am Clara's lover,' he wept. 'I was coming to meet her when I heard the scream and the commotion that followed. One of the servants told me – '

Zouch was going to strike him down, but a ghostly apparition appeared before them both. It told them that Neville was already dead, and pronounced judgement on them both. Lord Zouch, his wife and son, it said, would die in seven days, and for seven years at the September feast of Holyrood, his ghost must re-enact the tragedy, but with ringing footsteps to warn of his coming.

The monk was made to keep a vow of silence until the haunting ended.

And so it came to pass, exactly as the apparition had prophesized. Within a week Lord Zouch and his family were dead, and the castle rang to his ghostly footsteps for seven years. Then the monk related the story to all who would listen, before suddenly dying too, perhaps reunited with his sweetheart at last.

Rockingham Castle takes its name from the village of Rockingham, where the castle is located, as does Rockingham Forest. During the time of William the Conqueror it gained importance as a royal retreat. Many centuries later, Rockingham Castle was a popular haunt of writer Charles Dickens, who was a great friend of Richard and Levinia Watson, ancestors of the current family. The castle is the inspiration for Chesney Wold in one of his greatest works, Bleak House. *Today, the castle remains the private home of the Saunders Watson family. Access is granted at certain times of the year.*

THE CASTLE
OF DEATH

It was the end of January, in the Year of our Lord 1587, although *which* Lord was a matter of life and death, even for monarchs. Yet in the dead of night, the difference between a Catholic and a Protestant God could seem very slim indeed.

Fotheringhay Castle was a cold place, drear some might say, despite its charming location overlooking the bend of the sluggish Nene with its stone bridge and picturesque village beyond (its sleepily steady life a world away). It was bitterly cold that winter, and no amount of tapestries and fine rugs, thick cloaks and furs could keep out the chill – it got into your very bones.

The two guards standing outside the chamber of the royal prisoner watched their breath freeze in the wan torchlight of the passage. They shivered inside their chain mail and leather; stamped their feet to keep warm and flapped their arms. They caught each other doing this and rolled their eyes, sharing a laugh.

Suddenly, the torches guttered in their brackets, as though being licked, sending shadows skittering across the walls. A flame of bright fire appeared, as though stolen from the torches and gathered together, forming the suggestion of a figure, dazzlingly bright. The guards shielded their eyes and it vanished.

The men gasped, rubbed their eyes, looked at each other and shook their heads. Did you see what I saw, both their expressions read. It was fast approaching the witching hour: maybe their imaginations had run away with them? A trick of the wind? They laughed, their eyes white in the gloom of the passage.

Then, the fire-phantom appeared again, blinding them with its incandescence.

Eight days later, an event would take place in the castle that would change the course of English history.

On the evening of 7 February 1587, Mary was told that she was to be executed the next morning. She had been held captive in England for nineteen years. How ironic that she had fled to this cursed land for safety, hoping her sister, Elizabeth, would offer her sanctuary and help to reclaim her native throne. How wrong could she have been? Her sister had her kept under lock and key for many years, but always held off any final, irreversible act.

The capture and confession of Babington put an end to that. The plot to assassinate the Protestant Queen had been revealed, and one by one the conspirators had been sent to the block. Mary's royal head was the only one that was left. Her sister stayed her hand from signing the death warrant, nervous of the precedent that regicide might set, but in the end relented, despite the intercession of Scotland, France and Italy. 'So long as there is life in her, there is hope; so as they live in hope, we live in fear,' she reasoned.

And so the royal prisoner was informed of her imminent execution. The earls of Shrewsbury and Kent had arrived that very evening. Mary had expected it, and acted with grace and practicality. Eye-witnesses described how she spent the last hours of her life in prayer, distributing her belongings to her household, and writing her will and a letter to the King of France. Her little lapdog looked up at her with big eyes, sensing her mood, letting out a plaintive whine now and then, which Mary soothed away. The time for tears was over.

The fateful morning came. Mary prepared herself with the dignity of a queen and was led to the Great Hall. There, a scaffold had been erected, two-feet high and draped in black. This was to be her stage, where the last act of her life was to be performed. All she had to do was play her part.

The atmosphere in the room was heavy with anticipation. All eyes burned into her. Without faltering a step, she walked towards her doom.

Two, three steps and she was before the block, furnished with a cushion for her to kneel upon. Three stools were on the platform, for her and the earls of Shrewsbury and Kent, who sat there, ready to witness her execution.

The executioners (the giant hooded fellow named Bull and his scrawny bug-eyed assistant) knelt before her and asked forgiveness. She replied, her voice clipped and clear, 'I forgive you with all my heart, for now, I hope, you shall make an end of all my troubles.'

Her servants, Jane Kennedy and Elizabeth Curle, and the executioners helped Mary to remove her outer garments, revealing a velvet petticoat, satin bodice and a pair of sleeves all in dark red, the liturgical colour of martyrdom in the Catholic Church.

As she disrobed she smiled and said that she 'never had such grooms before, nor ever put off her clothes before such a company'. She was blindfolded by the kind but shaking hands of Kennedy, with a white veil embroidered in gold. Firm hands helped her kneel down on the cushion in front of the block. She positioned her head on the block and stretched out her arms. There, she uttered her last words: '*In manus tuas, Domine, commendo spiritum meum*'.*

She had become Queen of the Scots at the age of six. Now, at the age of forty-four, her reign had ended.

The Bull's grip wavered. His first blow missed the monarch's neck and struck the back of her head. Whether the executed or the witnesses let out a cry, is not recorded. The Bull extracted his axe and, under the stern glare of the earls, tried again. The second blow severed Mary's head, except for a small bit of sinew, which the executioner quickly spliced, like a butcher finishing a cut of meat.

The red blood poured out from the limp carcase onto the floor of the Great Hall.

As was the protocol, The Bull lifted her head aloft and declared 'God save the Queen'. At that moment, the auburn tresses in his hand turned out to be a wig and the head fell to the ground, revealing that Mary had very short, grey hair.

Then, an extraordinary thing: the Bull's assistant pulled at the fallen queen's garments, seeking to lift the body aside, when her little lapdog, a Skye terrier, which had been hiding among her skirts, appeared suddenly, barking wildly. Shaking and wild-eyed, it ran between the head and shoulders of its owner, and there stood its ground, covered in blood and gore. After a few bitten hands and curses it was removed by force, taken away and washed. What befell it after this is not recorded.

All of her clothing, the block, and everything touched by her blood, were burned in the fireplace of the Great Hall to obstruct relic-hunters.

After her death, a ghostly apparition – whether it was headless or not, the accounts do not specify – was seen following an underground passage from the castle to the oratory near Southwick Hall. Footsteps were quite audible, as was the creak of the door, then, the click-click of a rosary.

In the royal prisoner's chamber there was discovered writing on the sill, engraved with Mary's diamond ring: 'From the top of all my trust, mishap has laid me in the dust.'

By 1635, less than fifty years after the execution, Fotheringhay Castle – the birthplace of Richard III; death place of Mary, Queen of Scots – was reported to be in a ruinous state and was completely demolished soon afterwards.

For many years afterwards it was recorded by local people that strange music – ghostly drums and trumpets – could be heard coming from the remaining earthworks. In the 1950s, a policeman from Oundle went to investigate reports of 'disturbances' but found nothing. Stones from the castle were removed to help build the Talbot Inn at Oundle, which was reputedly haunted by Mary's ghost.

Fotheringhay has been called 'The saddest place in England'. With its windswept hill covered in wild grasses, making a lonely song, it certainly has a melancholic atmosphere. When I visited it was a sunny but windy day, and it felt bleak but beautiful. The final piece of masonry – imprisoned within iron railings – had a rag of tartan attached, a yellow rose, and a thistle. It feels poetic that the old mound of the castle is now covered in purple thistles – a little corner of Northamptonshire that is forever Scotland.
* 'Into thy hands, O Lord, I commend my spirit'.

THIRTY-SIX

THE
DUTCH DOLL

I still wake at night with the terrors –
the memory of that Thing has stayed
with me all my born days. Now, I am an
old woman, a Finedon girl through and
through, and the pictures of those days are
as fresh as ever.

I remember my first day there, standing
in front of the entrance of the old Girls
Charity School in my crisp new uniform,
clutching my satchel, biting my lip. It had
been on my mind all summer, now here
I was – one new face amid a flurry of
others, faces that would become known to
me over the coming term. There, looking
on the new intake with an air of superior-
ity, were Maria Hacksley, Sarah Durden
and Hannah Randall, like the three
witches from *Macbeth*. They inspected
everyone's satchel as they arrived, under
the pretence of friendship, so as not to
draw the eye of the playground supervi-
sor. They confiscated any sweets or pretty
things, as a 'tithe' to protect you against

the 'D.D.' – the Dutch Doll! We had heard rumours of it. It was the stuff of every Finedon schoolgirl nightmare. An old wooden doll, carved in the likeness of a girl dressed in the Charity School uniform. It was used as the ultimate threat against misbehaviour – the perpetrator would be forced to spend some time in a locked basement with it. Any who had the pleasure never misbehaved again.

The three witches swore they knew how to ward off its evil – they had a 'special arrangement' with it and could turn it against any who wronged them, or failed to pay up. One by one, the new arrivals left their welcoming committee in tears. I was no better than the rest, starting the day in sniffles, the cold truth at how cruel the world was slowly sinking in, all my hopes dashed.

'We'll be keeping an eye on you! And if we miss something, D.D. won't!' they cackled.

We shuffled to school assembly and were given a stern introduction to the school by its headmistress, Ms Kay – a formidable woman who would have no truck with nonsense. 'This is a respectable school. There is over a hundred years of tradition at Finedon. All those former pupils who have gone onto shining lives as housewives, schoolmistresses, governesses, and clergywomen look down upon you. Do not let them down!'

I fitted in as best I could and studied hard, learning my three R's, the history of England, French, embroidery, handwriting, and so on. Keep your head down. Don't stand out. That was the common survival strategy. Don't attract the attention of the three witches.

Once in a while we were let out. On holidays we would run rampant around the streets of Finedon, chasing or being chased by boys through smelly Shitten Alley, where the refuse cart is kept; and running the gauntlet of the Tainty – the Tenters Yard – in and out of the newly milled cloths hanging there, smelling fresh. I would be the dutiful daughter and visit my elderly relatives, running errands helping mother. The land there was a magical place then. You could go off with a bottle of pop and a bun and be happy out in the fields all day, knowing no harm would come to you. Everyone knew everyone else and strangers stood out like a sore thumb.

But all the while the Charity School loomed like a tombstone, and we knew we would have to go back there and face the witches and the D.D.

Then one day, the three witches played a cruel trick on me. 'Goody Two Shoes' they called me. Truth was they were green-eyed at my good grades. And so they set me up – they placed a frog in my desk. It made me squeal so that the teacher, Grumpy Drawers, demanded that I was sent to the headmistress after I refused to return to my seat. Ms Kay was very disappointed to see me in her office, and I tried to explain what had happened but I was beside myself with fright, and so, to make it worse, Ms Kay sent me to the cellar to sober up. An hour with the Dutch Doll should put some sense into your head.

How I wailed then, with hot tears and snot streaking my face. I was led by the caretaker down to the cellar and left there with a short candle. The locked clicked behind me with a sickening finality.

The silence was thick, like a heavy coat. The candle guttered in its little saucer, frail, yet casting twitching phantoms of light and dark against the dank walls. I couldn't look, but I knew I must. Out of the corner of my eye I could see the feet, with little black wooden shoes. I raised my head and there, caught in the candle glare, was the Dutch Doll – prim and proper, looking at me with those dead eyes. All alone together. Was it my imagination, or did it seem to come alive? I screamed to be let out, but my cries fell on deaf ears.

How I survived that hour I do not know.

When I was finally let out I was silent. I could not speak.

Unable to reveal the names of my tormentors I was led back to the classroom. The three witches gave me evil looks, but when they weren't called up they nodded approvingly, with sickly smiles they made me one of theirs. My ordeal gave me some kudos, and for not 'grassing' on the three witches, I was made an honorary member of their gang.

Yet their cruelty did not stop. They delighted in making the young 'uns squirm with tales of how the D.D. had its legs cut off, to stop it walking around at night. I knew this was not true, but I did not tell. I barely spoke and was nicknamed 'Ghost'.

Then, one day, the three witches went too far. Grumpy Drawers had had enough and sent them all the Ms Kay for the cane. In revenge, they sneaked into the cellar, stole the D.D. and attached it to the door of Grumpy's classroom by string, so that when it was opened, it would swing out. This it did, to such devastating effect that Grumpy had a 'turn' and had to be given a week off work.

This time, the culprits could not hide their identity. They were summoned before Ms Kay and expelled. Many of us cheered when they left, although they turned and swore revenge. 'No one will protect you from the D.D. now!' We hid, avoiding their evil eye, but secretly smiling.

They lurked around the school gates for a few weeks after that, throwing stones and making cat calls at us, but we knew their lives had been ruined before they had properly begun. Without proper education they were destined to be skivvies and ale-wives.

I got my diploma and made a life for myself, but I never forgot the Dutch Doll. The school was eventually sold into private hands. The doll was moved to the local church when the school moved to another village. And there it remained, looking out over the parishioners, no longer seeming such a figure of terror. How could we have been so foolish?

Finedon, or Thingdon (listed in the Domesday Book as Tingdene, from the Old English words þing meaning assembly or meeting and Denu meaning valley or vale), is a village and a parish in the Wellingborough district of Northampton. The details of the doll, Ms Kay and the three girls being expelled are all true. The narrator is invented but based upon local women who remembered the doll with some dread. The doll was kept in the church when the school moved but it was stolen in 1981. Local people were angry and upset. News clippings warned of the consequences to the thieves. The police still have not traced the object of terror.

THIRTY-SEVEN

THE CHAPEL
OUT OF TIME

Mr H.G. Lee was a very punctilious fellow. He liked things to be 'proper', his world to be neat and orderly. His trousers were always ironed, his shirt crisp and white, his tie knotted tightly, his short hair combed over in a sober manner, and his briefcase slim and professional. He was a school inspector, working in the county in the late 1940s.

One lunch hour, in between school visits, Mr Lee decided to go to a church in the area, recommended to him because of its architecture. 'Catch it while you can,' his friend had advised, 'for they are modernising the church interior.'

Mr Lee had a penchant for church architecture. It was orderly and purposeful. Everything had its place. Viewing it made him feel peaceful, away from the din of the schoolyard, the scruffy tired buildings and exhausted teachers. He sought out the church as dark clouds gathered overhead.

The school inspector was oblivious to this, lost in contemplation of the gargoyles, which reminded him of some of the pupils he had had the misfortune to come into contact with. He hated running the gauntlet of the playground and tried to time his inspections to coincide with lessons, so he could slip in and out without mixing with the hoi polloi of pupils.

Then a thunderstorm rudely broke – a flash made him blink, and then a crack split the sky very soon afterwards. Within moments, it was lashing down and he dashed for the vestibule.

He shook over his coat and brushed down his hat, tutting as he entered the cool interior. As his eyes adjusted and Mr Lee noted, with some satisfaction, that the much-despised modernisations clearly hadn't taken place. The notoriously uncomfortable pews had not been replaced. The most modern furniture he could see was the Jacobean-era stone pulpit. There was not even an organ visible. The place looked and felt as though it was stuck in a time warp, unchanged by the busy century outside.

He sat down on a hard wooden chair by the font, feeling at peace, when his reverie was disturbed by a voice, which echoed around the chapel: 'So, you are interested in our fine old church?'

Mr Lee started at the voice, and it took a moment to calm the beat of his heart. Composing himself, he turned to see a middle-aged clergyman in a cassock. Surely it must be the parish vicar, his white mutton-chop sideburns bracketed his round face and his whole bearing spoke of moral rectitude and a comfortable position in society.

Mr Lee got up and made his acquaintance, shaking hands. He noticed that the vicar's hands were cold – unusually so. Indeed, they sent a shiver down his back. He agreed with the reverend, adding that he thought the church the best preserved in the county.

Brushing an imaginary crumb from his cassock, the man of the cloth, who didn't give his name, sighed. 'We have seen troubled times, and some churches have suffered great damage. But I trust in the Lord Protector to see that my beautiful church is safe from harm.'

Mr Lee was puzzled at this. Surely, he must have misheard – 'Lord Protector?'

'Yes. You see, the Lord Protector is an old friend of mine. We were at college together.'

Mr Lee frowned at this, but he did not wish to accuse the vicar of foolishness or fabulation. He was somewhat relieved when the priest offered to take him on a tour of the church, pointing out its modest charms. The School Inspector assumed a countenance of polite interest, but he was troubled. Was the fellow deranged? Sometimes, these provincial priests could be a little … eccentric.

Eventually, the weather cleared and a sunbeam pierced the stained-glass window, illuminating the gloomy interior.

'Ah, looks like the tempest has passed. I must be on my way. This has been most, most interesting.'

The priest showed the visitor to the door. They passed out into the sunlight, their shoes crunching on the gravel path. For once, Mr Lee felt overwhelmingly relieved to be in the light and the air. He looked up at the serene clouds, breathing a deep sigh. An aeroplane passed

noisily overheard, ruining the moment. He went to make a comment to the vicar, only to discover, to his surprise, that he stood alone in the graveyard. Slightly puzzled he walked back into the church. He didn't want to leave without saying goodbye. The fellow had been most generous with his time and knowledge after all.

Mr Lee gasped. The interior of the church looked completely different. He checked – had he come in through the same door?

An unsightly modern organ masked the beautiful chapel arch he had admired earlier. The whole acoustic ambience of the place was different and, come to think of it, he didn't remember hearing the vicar's footsteps on the cold stone floor.

A noticeboard, which had not been apparent before, listed all the incumbent vicars of the church, and Mr Lee scanned the list. His eyes rolled down to 1640 and 1650 – the mention of the Lord Protector had niggled him. He made a note of the name of the parson who served then.

Calling into the silence and finding no reply, he left.

Later, he followed up his research, for the strange visit to the church had played on his mind, lingering in his imagination for several days afterwards. The vanishing priest particularly troubled him. He discovered that the parson who had served during the Civil War had been educated at Sidney Sussex College, Cambridge, in 1616, where Oliver Cromwell, the Lord Protector, had studied. The Lord Protector had left in June 1617 without taking a degree, immediately after the death of his father. His head was eventually to be buried there.

This curious story was passed on to the late folklorist Katherine Briggs, and related in Mysterious Northamptonshire by Peter Hill. The location of the church is, frustratingly, not specified.

THIRTY EIGHT

THE
ENCLOSED POET

The old man sat in the portico of All Saints' Church, watching the passers-by. Northampton moved busily around him – traders and shoppers going back and forth up Gold Street opposite, the Drapery to his right, down Bridge Street to his left. The clip-clop of horse-shoes on cobbles, the rattle of carriages and wagons, the rough cries of traders from the market, the chatter of housewives, the squeals of laughter of a gang of grubby children playing with a hoop in the gutter, the bawling of a baby, a blind fiddler scraping out a tune for a few pennies, a peal of bells ringing out from the tower – a living sea of waking noise swirling about him.

He took out his pencil stub and a scrap of paper – a handbill for some 'Nine Day Wonder' passing through town, like him. He laid his head in a strange kind of hostelry. They fed and watered him, gave him a bed in his very own room. Now and then they would ask him peculiar questions; sometimes even prod and probe him. Men of learning would come and gawp, and talk about him as though he was not there. A woman came once, claiming to be his wife. But that was ridiculous, for he was wedded to Mary at Hinton, his childhood sweetheart, and none other. Yet she still had not visited after all these years. There must be a very good reason, he convinced himself – ill-health, business in Stamford, a bad road … Whenever he could he would come and sit here and scan the crowds, hoping to see her coming up the road in a

pretty bonnet, calling out to him in delight when she sees him. Sometimes, he swears he sees her and quickly writes a poem for her, thrusting it into the hand of a passing lady. He writes and writes and writes, pouring out his heart.

There was a time when he thought his head was empty, and the men in frock coats had taken away all his letters. But, there was an undying spring in him. The words just welled up. He couldn't stop them. It was as natural to him as breathing. He had been a rhymer all of his life. Had a talent for it. Even the good folk in London had said so, for a while.

Honest John they used to call him, as well as Boney Parte, Madbad Byron, Boxer Jack, and Billy Shakespeare. He's been them all. There'd been parades and processions. He'd been wreathed in laurels, gold and flowers. The crowds had cheered him through the streets. Yet, all he had ever wanted was Mary's smile, a kiss from her hawthorn-berry lips. It had all been for her.

The old man got up and walked. He was suddenly filled with fire. He would walk to Hinton right now – not stop until he saw its spire, until he walked up her path and knocked on her door and saw her face and kissed her lips.

With determined gait, he set out, striding across the cobbles.

He had walked once from Epping Forest all the way home; slept on the sides of the road and got so hungry he ate grass. Yet, by thunder, he had got all the way home. Gave his wife a turn, so he did, turning up like that, out of the blue, looking so ragged. He had been out of his mind – but now, now he was back amid fields he knew like the back of his hand. He was home. The land of his mind.

The old man stopped on the brow of Bridge Street hill, wondering where he was going. For a moment he was a little confused. He looked about him. Saw All Saints'. The clock. His stomach rumbled. Soon be tea time – time to make his way back to his nice room, where they looked after him so. An important poet. Their writer-in-residence.

John Clare, the so-called Peasant Poet, was admitted to the Northampton General Lunatic Hospital and Asylum (now St Andrews – the largest psychiatric hospital in Europe) on 29 December 1841. There he remained until his death on 20 May 1864. For a man who had grown up under the wide skies and unimpeded horizons of the unenclosed Fens (witnessing the Enclosure's Act of 1820 first-hand) being so interred must have been hell on earth, however good-intentioned was his time there. The asylum was run in an enlightened way (for the period) by a Dr Pritchard, who helped pay for Clare's own room (as a private patient) and allowed him to wander the town. He would fre-

*quently sit in the portico of All Saints' Church and talk to passers-by,
handing out his poems (who knows how many were lost that way?).
He wrote some of his most poignant poems in the town, including
his heartrending 'I Am' – perhaps the most touching evocation of
mental illness ever written. By the time he came to Northampton
his was a broken mind – a butterfly smashed on the wheel of society – but what genius occasionally glimmered there still, glimpsed
in scribbled fragments. Growing up in the town, Clare was a great
inspiration. Even though his time in the town was not a happy one,
to have such a literary exemplar in my neck of the woods meant a lot.
I took part in bicentenary celebrations in 1993, reading out Clare's
verse around the town with fellow Northampton poets. My poem
about Clare ('I am my dear Mary') was one of the first ones of mine
published, in their second collection,* Stealing Ivy. *I researched Clare
a great deal for my first novel, visiting Helpston and spending time
in the local studies section of the central library, with his death mask.
Clare's tragic story speaks for all those whose talent has been neglected
or ill-treated; for the quiet charms of the Fens; and for all the
'voiceless' beings of nature, for whom Clare was such an observant,
eloquent, and impassioned ambassador. As a fiddle player, like his
father, and recorder of folk customs (in* The Midsummer Cushion
and The Shepherd's Calendar*) Clare was an important part of the
folk tradition of the area; and his own tragic life, in its many retell-
ings, has become the stuff of folktale.*

Appendices

Fairy
Fluff

The Fairy Faith in Northamptonshire lingered until at least the times of the mid-nineteenth century, when it was noted by Sternberg in *The Dialect and Folklore of Northamptonshire* (1851) that 'The faith is in its last stage of decay'. He rather poetically adds the problem the collector has at acquiring scraps of folklore in their evanescence: 'Steam-threshing machines have long superseded the magic flail of the drudging goblin; and even the dancing-grounds of Queen Mab and her tiny lieges are menaced by the sacrilegious coulters of patent ploughs.' Here, I have collected some of the tales that have survived.

The Fairy and the Thresher

A good farmer called Hodge, engaged in the hard work of threshing – back-breaking stuff – was baffled by the speed at which his sheaves vanished. No sooner had he stacked his stooks, bent back to his work, then they dwindled away. Though he worked slow and steady, his sheaves toppled quicker. Puzzled by this, but wishing to prevent it, the farmer had extra bolts placed on his doors and a man stationed in the yard to watch.

Alas, each morning they found the fastenings untouched and a telling absence amongst the 'mow'.

Hodge was determined to catch the culprit and he hid in the barn all night, amid the sheaves, trying not to sneeze. At midnight, two tiny elves appeared popping up through a pike-hole. They set about working away at the sheaves, reducing them to a size that would fit through the hole. They tidily made them into minute bundles.

Hodge, though he did not like what he saw, watched on in fascination. After a while, they paused to mop their brows. One spoke in a squeaky voice: 'I twit; do you twit?'

The farmer, unable to stop himself, cried out 'The Devil twit ye!' He rushed out. 'I'll twit ye if ye bent off!'

The sheave-thieves got the message, and taking frit, they up sticks and flitted down the pike-hole.

And that was the last he saw of them.

Job done!

This tale was recorded in Sternberg's classic text of 1851. It cites John Clare's long poem of rural life, 'Village Minstrel', which describes the Good Folk:

Mice are not reckon'd greater thieves,
They take away as well as eat,
And still the housewife's eyes they cheat:
In spite of all the folks that swarm,
In cottage small, and larger farm,
They through each keyhole pop and pop,
Like wasps into a grocer's shop.

FAIRY FOOTBALL

Once, in the south of the county, there was a young fellow who was lucky enough to witness a rare sporting fixture: fairy football.

The moon was as full and round as, well, a football, on the night the young man in question made his way home from a neighbouring village, somewhat in his cups, for he had been making merry all day on feast-day. He found himself stumbling into a commotion – a crowd of wee folk, divided into two teams, were fiercely contending for a football. So merry was he that he did not find it unusual, but instead joined in the match with great fervour. With delight he belted the ball a good 'un, but to his dismay it burst with a tremendous wallop and all the fairy footballers vanished in an instant. The impact of the explosion left him stunned on the ground, in the cold mud, in the middle of the night, sobering him up somewhat rapidly.

He scratched his poor old head – what had just happened? Was it all a dream? He staggered to his feet and went to walk home, but something gleaming caught his eye – the burst ball had scattered golden coins all across the field!

He had some fun picking all of those up, blessing the fairy footballers as he did.

Northampton's own football team is nicknamed the 'Cobblers', and they seemed to live up to their name when I was growing up there. Maybe they could have had some training with these fellows?

More Mischief

Once, a young fellow, enamoured by a farmer's wife, goes a-lurking outside her bedroom window. He is amazed to discover said wife and husband off 'sporting on calfs' – raising hell like a couple of witches, on the backs of alarmed young Jerseys. He finds himself caught up in one of these nocturnal sorties – the purpose, to steal a child to be used in some dastardly ceremony no doubt.

Prior to his accompanying them he is made to swear not to utter the sacred name of Him Upstairs – a name accursed to all creatures of the night.

And so the three of them rode off, but the young man was not accustomed to riding on such a steed. The young cow gave him problems, so he involuntarily called out the Lord's name, which caused them to pause and warn him.

Their steeds carried them at great speed across the land. They seemed to fly through the air and shrink down to a minute size, to pass through keyholes. One, two, but the third – the door of the infant's room – made the young man quake with fear. 'God save us!' he called out, thus ruining their plans. He was blasted back to where he started, but the baby was saved.

Sternberg suggests that this tale resembles the Irish legend of the 'Master and Man'. In brief, a man becomes servant of a Cluricaune, and assists his master in an attempt to abduct a young lady about to be wed. While lying in wait for their unsuspecting prey, the bride-to-be sneezes, and the man (called Pat), unable to resist the force of habit, says 'bless you!' – twice. This destroys their chances but saves the girl.

THE DEVIL MAKES WORK

A farmer had to go off on business for a week. He gave strict instructions to his lads to spread manure on a certain field, awaiting there in steaming heaps. With the gaffer gone, the lads thought no more of muck-spreading, but got down to the important business of doing bugger all.

On the day of the master's return, one of the young idlers suddenly remembered the task appointed them and became afeared. He lay on the ground, bemoaning his lot. 'What am I going to do? I am lost!'

Just then, a funny little old man appeared – wizened like a walnut, wielding a blackthorn stick. 'What's the matter, my lad?' he asked in a soft voice.

'I bent done me wurk, zur,' sobbed the no-good-lad.

'Never you mind, master bone-idle. Can you run?'

The lad replied, 'Eez, zur.'

'Then off with you to that stile over the far end. And if I do the work and beat you to it, then you'll be mine!'

The speech somewhat gave away the true nature of the old man. But the fear of the farmer's punishment when he returned was greater, and so he agreed. So off he dashed, going hell-for-leather. The soil flew all across the field in a flurry of slurry and soon the field was covered: the old man pelting after him like a hare.

The boy raced with all his youthful speed, until he felt his heart would burst – the old man chuffing away at his heels. But the boy beats him to the stile – leaps it, feeling the burning grasp of his devilish adversary on his smock.

From the other side of the fence, the boy laughs at the old man, who stamps up and down before vanishing in a puff of sulphur.

The farmer returned by evening, satisfied to see his work done. He rewarded the boy. Maybe the lad wasn't such a ne'er-do-well after all. But in the morning, the muck was back in little heaps again, and the boy got a tanning.

The Fairies' Farewell

Sternberg, travelling the county in the sensible mid-nineteenth century, pursuing his gentlemanly pursuit of folktale collecting, asked a 'rustic' local, 'What has become of all these spirits?'

'What, arnt you heerd?' he replied.

'No.'

'Why then, I'll tell 'e. A long time ago, the passons all laid their yeads togither and hiked 'em off to the Red Saa!'

BIBLIOGRAPHY

Briggs, Katherine, *A Sampler of British Folktales* (Routledge & Kegan, 1977)

Codd, Daniel, *Mysterious Northamptonshire* (Breedon Books Publishing, 2009)

Dack, Charles, *Weather and Folklore* (Peterborough Natural History, Scientific and Archaeological Society, 1911)

'Folklore and Legends of Britain' in *Reader's Digest*, 1973

Forward, Eleanor J., 'Place-names of the Whittlewood area, Eleanor J. Forward, BA, Thesis submitted to the University of Nottingham, for the degree of Doctor of Philosophy, September 2007'

Greenall, R.L., *A History of Northamptonshire* (Phillmore, 1979)

Grimes, Dorothy A., *Like Dew Before the Sun: Life and Language in Northamptonshire* (Published Privately, 1991)

Hill, Peter, *Folklore of Northamptonshire* (The History Press, 2005)

Hill, Peter, *In Search of the Green Man in Northamptonshire* (Orman, 1996)

Hill, Peter, *Secret Northamptonshire* (Amberley Publishing, 2009)

Pegg, John, 'Landscape Analysis and Appraisal Church Stowe, Northamptonshire, as a Candidate Site for the Battle of Watling Street', 2010

Poole, Gary, and Karen Stokes, *The Witches of Northamptonshire* (The History Press, 2006)

Pipe, Marian, *Ghosts and Folklore of Northamptonshire* (Speigl Press, 1986)

Pipe, Marian, *Mysteries and Memorials of Northamptonshire* (Speigl Press, 1987)

Pipe, Marian, *Myths and Legends of Northamptonshire* (Speigl Press, 1985)

Pipe, Marian, *Tales of Northamptonshire* (Countryside Books, 1990)

Sternberg, Thomas, *The Dialect and Folklore of Northamptonshire* (SR Publications, 1971)

Story, Alfred T., *Historical Legends of Northamptonshire* (John Taylor, 1880)

Swift, Eric, *Folk Tales of the East Midland* (Thomas Nelson & Sons Ltd, 1954)

The Restless Ghost (John Millet, Taylor and Son, 1878)

'The Rebellion of Boudicca' episode of *Battlefield Britain* (BBC, 2004)

INDEX

ENDNOTE BY KEVAN MANWARING

The county of Northamptonshire has embraced diverse influences for centuries – Celtic, Roman, Saxon, Norse, Norman, and so on. Since the twentieth century (in particular, post-war Britain) this multi-cultural melting pot has been further enriched by waves of immigrants who have settled here, bringing their excitingly exotic blend of flavours, music, languages, customs, skills and tales, and whose children, grandchildren and great-grandchildren have become born and bred Northamptonians. As my own family (on my father's side) was part of this experience, I am all too aware of the many colourful narratives awaiting to be told – Afro-Caribbean, Irish, Indian, traveller, Chinese, Polish and other Eastern European influences, to name a few. These and other contemporary folk tales from all walks of life deserve to be collected (what is a community but an interlacement of narratives?). And if this current collection inspires local groups to do so, then I will be happy.